THE AUTHORS

Eric Jacobs has worked in Whitehall and Fleet Street for many years, writing on political and industrial affairs for *The Guardian* and *The Sunday Times*. He wrote the leading articles for *Today* throughout its first five years and is the author of *Stop Press: the Inside Story of The Times Dispute*. With Robert Worcester he co-authored *We British: Britain under the MORIscope*, published in 1990.

Robert Worcester is chairman of MORI. He is the author of *British Public Opinion: A Guide to the History and Methodology of Political Opinion Polling in Great Britain;* co-author of *Private Opinions – Public Polls*; editor of *Political Opinion Polling: an International Review*; and co-editor of *Political Communications* and *The Consumer Market Research Handbook.* He is Honorary Visiting Professor at City University, London.

TYPICALLY
BRITISH?

The Prudential MORI Guide

TYPICALLY BRITISH?

The Prudential MORI Guide

Eric Jacobs and Robert Worcester

BLOOMSBURY

First published 1991 by Bloomsbury Publishing Limited,
2 Soho Square, London W1V 5DE

Copyright © 1991 by Eric Jacobs and Robert Worcester

A CIP record for this book is available from the British Library

ISBN 0 7475 1102 0

Designed and typeset by Aztec Press
Charts by Turningpoint Design
Printed by Clays Limited, St Ives plc

CONTENTS

INTRODUCTION

Did you know that...
- Nearly one adult in five has lived with someone as though they were married and one in 20 – nearly 2½ million people – is doing so right now.
- The quality that most men and women find attractive in each other is a sense of humour.
- One person in 100 over the age of 55 still hankers after someone they knew at 15 and still hopes to marry him or her.
- The three jobs that the most people wanted just before they were free to leave school were to run their own business, to become a nurse or to join the armed forces.
- More people in Britain go to museums and art exhibitions than to football matches or pop concerts.
- Britain's favourite dish is the Sunday roast.
- The four top concerns of the British in 1991 are crime, the National Health Service, unemployment and pollution.

This is the kind of information you get - and only can get - from opinion polling. Which is why surveys like *Typically British?* have become the true barometers of our age.

Politicians and businessmen peer eagerly into polls to see how their policies and products are going down with the public.

But that public, with no axe to grind and nothing to sell, is just as interested. Opinion polling tells them how they stand and how they compare. It lets them know how others like them are thinking, feeling, behaving. It reveals just how like or unlike their fellow citizens they really are.

Strangely, though, there is no independent, easily accessible research conducted and published for no other reason than to inform, guide, and, not least, entertain the public. That is because polling is usually done for special interest groups, like those politicians and businessmen, not for the interest of the public.

Typically British? will, we believe, fill that gap. We intend it to be the first in an annual series of guides to public opinion in Britain. Year by year we will look at different facets of British behaviour, attitudes, opinions, values. And as the years go by we will return to old subjects to see how opinion has changed.

It will, we believe, grow richer with the years. Although the British have been polled for more than half a century now, it is astonishing how few direct comparisons it is possible to make with what people thought on any issue ten, let alone 20 or 30, years ago. There is a mountain of information on demographic trends like movements in employment and wages or births and death, but precious little to tell us about the movement of people's feelings towards those things. This is another gap we hope to fill.

In this first issue we begin by exploring the ever-fascinating relationships between the sexes in **Love, Sex, Marriage**. We then look at how people's early dreams have worked out in practice and what ambitions they still hope to achieve, in **Hopes, Dreams, Achievements**. Next, we examine **The British Way of Life**: how people spend their spare time, what healthy and not so healthy habits they have, who prefers opera to football. After that we assess **The Mood of the Nation**: how happy, confident and optimistic the British people are. We also take a look at **Britain in the World** - what do people think of the country in which they live and what do they think about Britain's place in the larger world? Then, we offer some **Portraits of the Nation**. These summarise the attitudes of the ages and the sexes in simple, easy to read digests. If you are a woman under 35 or a man over 65 - or any other combination of age and sex - just turn to this section and see how you compare with others like, or unlike, yourself. Finally, for those who are interested in the detail of how polling works, we print in full our questionnaire, including the principal findings of our survey.

We would like to express our gratitude to the Prudential Corporation for funding our research. Without its generous help, *Typically British?* would not have been possible. We should make it clear, however, that the Prudential is in no way responsible for the contents of this book. The survey was entirely our design and so was its interpretation. Any errors, faults or defects are entirely down to us, not the Pru.

We would also like to thank Peter Hutton and Richard White of MORI for their assiduous help at every stage of the book's development, from their original ideas to their scrupulous checking of our text.

Reader's Note

We have tried to keep *Typically British?* as free of jargon as possible. But two technicalities need to be explained. When we talk about High, Medium and Low incomes we mean earnings of, respectively, £25,000 a year or more; between £11,500 and £25,000; and below £11,500.

When we talk about people's social class we mean - except where otherwise explained - class as defined by the opinion research industry.

This divides population into groups: A; B; C1; C2; D; E. For practical purposes, we put the ABC1s together as a single category, the middle class. They range from senior executives and professionals like doctors and lawyers to more junior white-collar workers, nurses, journalists and technicians. To make a comparison with an easily-understood hierachy, ABC1s include all the military ranks from Field Marshal to Sergeant, and represent 40% of Britain's population.

C2s are skilled and qualified manual workers – plumbers, electricians, heavy-goods vehicle drivers, bricklayers, printers and police constables – in military terms lance corporal to corporal.

Ds are semi-skilled workers - construction and farm labourers, waiters and waitresses and the army's privates.

Es are those people who live entirely from State benefit: like some single parents, pensioners and the unemployed: army privates retired.

C2s and DEs are the working classes, and account for 60% of the British.

People who have no qualifications or earnings of their own - for example, full-time housewives or other non-employed members of a family - are assigned the social class of their head of household.

For more details see **British Activists** at the end of the book. The questionnaire is also produced in full for reference.

Technical Note

MORI interviewed a representative quota sample of 1,230 people aged 15+ in 113 constituency sampling points throughout Great Britain. Interviews were conducted face-to-face, in-home, between 11 April and 2 May 1991. Data are weighted to reflect the known population profile. This size and design of sample we would expect nineteen times in twenty to be accurate to plus or minus three per cent. That is, have a sampling tolerance of $\pm 3\%$. For example, if we found, as we did, that 57% of our sample said they were married, there would be a 95% probability that the true percentage of married people aged 15 and over throughout Great Britain would be between 54% and 60%, with the greatest probability that the true figure is 57%.

London
August 1991

Eric Jacobs
and Robert Worcester

1 • LOVE, SEX, MARRIAGE

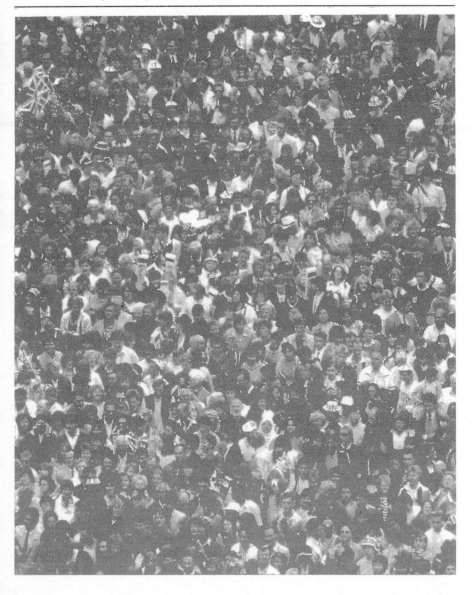

1 • LOVE, SEX, MARRIAGE

The battle of the sexes is worldwide and endless. But it has its local skirmishes too. We start our survey of the British battlefield by looking at how the sexes line up for the contest.

The Typically British Adult
- If you're British and over 15 you are most likely to be married.
- You are next most likely to be still single.
- Then, in descending order of probability, you are widowed, living with someone as though you were married, divorced, separated or single but engaged.

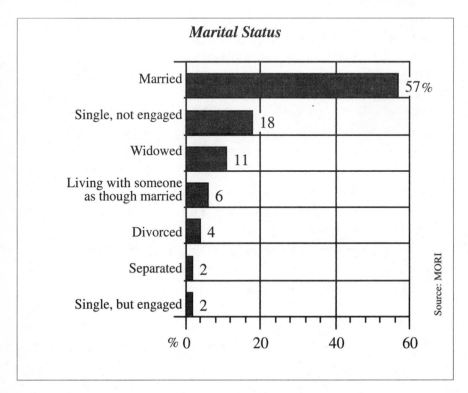

Now we will look at the make-up of these groups in more detail.

The Married

Just over half of adults are married – 57%. On the facing page are the proportions of married people in each of the groups into which we break down the population.

It may seem odd, or even downright impossible, that a higher proportion of men are married than of women. But there is a simple explanation. Women live longer than men and so are more likely to survive their husbands to become widows.

Almost one woman in six (17%) has lost her husband through death, making four times as many widows as widowers. Men whose wives have died make up only one in 25 (4%) of adult males.

The Singles

These are people who have not yet married and therefore cannot come into the categories of the divorced or separated. Nor are they currently engaged to be married or living with a partner.

Nearly one in five of adults – 18% – come into this category.

Not surprisingly, most single people are young. Four in ten of the under-35s are single and currently uncommitted to a partner.

But being single is not the same as being alone. Many singles have children living with them. Of those households that contain children the largest proportion – 70% – is headed by married people. But the second largest number – 14% of the total – is headed by a single person, usually a woman. (see chart overleaf).

Widows and Widowers

This is the next largest group, accounting for one in ten of all adults (11%), or around 4.5 million people.

As we have said, most are women and elderly. Only one woman in 50 (2%) under the age of 55 is a widow. But nearly one in three – 31% – of women over that age have lost their husbands.

Living Together

These are people who live together as if they were married in most respects except the formality of a marriage licence.

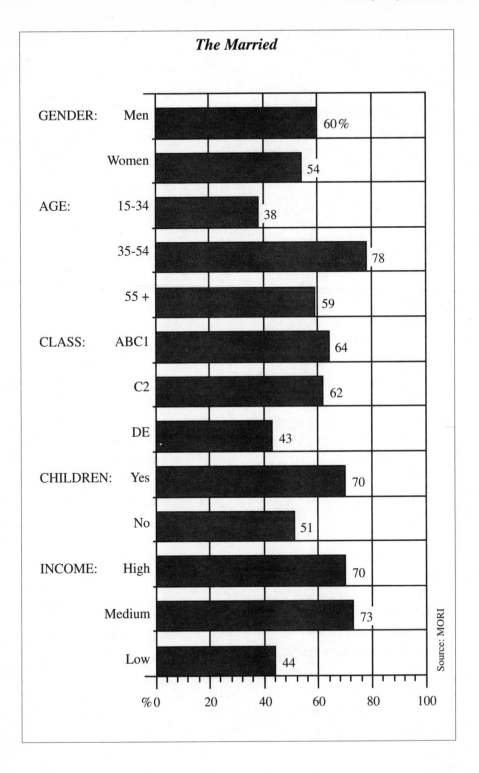

The Married

GENDER: Men — 60%
Women — 54
AGE: 15-34 — 38
35-54 — 78
55 + — 59
CLASS: ABC1 — 64
C2 — 62
DE — 43
CHILDREN: Yes — 70
No — 51
INCOME: High — 70
Medium — 73
Low — 44

%0 · 20 · 40 · 60 · 80 · 100

Source: MORI

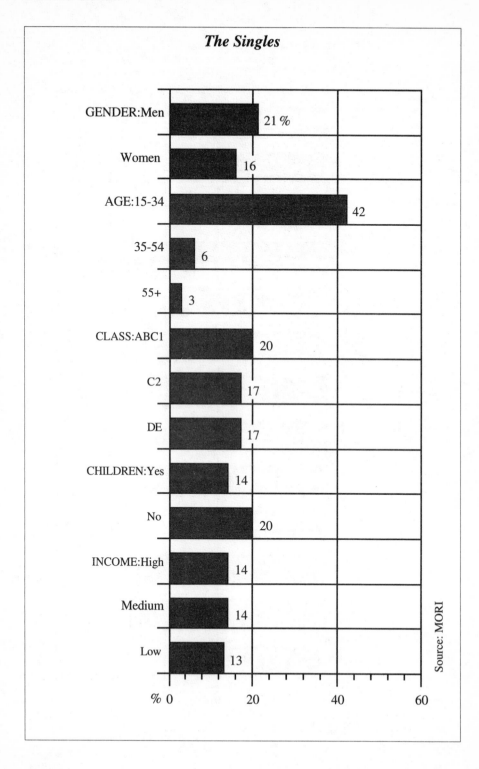

The Singles

GENDER:Men	21%
Women	16
AGE:15-34	42
35-54	6
55+	3
CLASS:ABC1	20
C2	17
DE	17
CHILDREN:Yes	14
No	20
INCOME:High	14
Medium	14
Low	13

% 0   20   40   60

Source: MORI

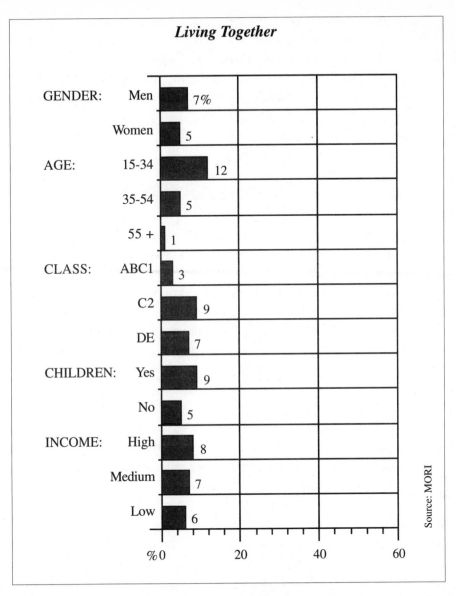

Living Together

		7%
GENDER:	Men	7%
	Women	5
AGE:	15-34	12
	35-54	5
	55 +	1
CLASS:	ABC1	3
	C2	9
	DE	7
CHILDREN:	Yes	9
	No	5
INCOME:	High	8
	Medium	7
	Low	6

%0   20   40   60

Source: MORI

It is a way of life widespread in Britain today. One in 20 adults (6%) – and one in nine of 15–34 year-olds now live in this form of relationship.

Close to 2¹/₂ million people are now living together. But if this looks like being a permanent feature of the British way of life, that does not make it a stable one.

With one of the highest divorce rates in Europe, British marriage is notorious for its instability. The state of living together is even more so.

For every person now living this way, almost three times as many have tried it only to separate from their partners. Nearly one adult in six – 16% of all adults – has lived with someone at some time in the past. A different person, that is, to anybody they might be living with now. And of those people currently living with a partner, nearly half – 40% – have already lived with another person.

Other features of living together
- More men claim to be living with a partner or to have lived with one than women (17% to 15%). But more men (4%) also declined to answer that question than women (2%). These differences may be accounted for by gay relationships.
- Living together is predominantly the lifestyle of young people. Only one in ten (9%) of the over–55s have tried it, against one in five (22%) of the under-35s.
- But it is not, as some imagine, the lifestyle of the careless young with plenty of money and the freedom to choose a series of partners. Those living together are just as likely to be on low incomes, to be lower on the social scale and to be council house tenants than they are to be high earners, high on the social scale or living in their own homes.

The Divorced

This is the fifth largest group of adults by marital status in Britain. At least one in 25 people – 4% – have tried marriage and failed.

Equal numbers of the divorced are men and women. And 2% of households with children in them are now headed by a divorced person.

Separated and Singles who are Engaged

These groups are too small at 2% each of the adult population to reveal many very significant characteristics. Though the singles who are engaged are, as we might expect, nearly all under 35.

The picture we have uncovered so far may look like a bleak one for marriage, with so many people now living in other ways.

But three-quarters of adult Britons have already tried marriage or intend to and most of those who haven't are still young enough to take their chance.

There's a lot of mileage left in marriage yet, as we shall see. First, though, we will look at what precedes it, at the mysterious process of attraction.

What men like in women – and women in men

Marriages don't just happen. Nor are they usually arranged.

Few people in Britain today have marriages planned for them by parents or match-makers. Who marries whom is something individuals settle for themselves on the basis of mutual attraction.

Why people feel attracted to each other is an eternal puzzle. Everyone who has ever set out to make a date with a stranger knows the truth of that all too well. Even as the telephone rings, the same agonising questions occur: what exactly does a man see in a woman, or a woman in a man? And have I got whatever it is the other sex is looking for?

Before getting on to marriage itself we thought we'd try to explore some of this strange territory of attraction. Not only for the benefit of those of courting years but for all age groups, since attraction is something people may feel all their lives.

We drew up a list of 15 things covering a wide range of physical, mental and emotional qualities, then asked our respondents to tell us which three or four of them they thought men most liked in women and women most liked in men.

This way we were able to discover which characteristics each sex thought most important in the other and at the same time to find out what both thought the opposite sex saw in them.

The order in which men and women ranked the qualities on our list can be found on the next two pages.

On one thing at least we can immediately see that practically everyone agrees. On all sides, having a sense of humour is highly regarded, whether people are talking about what they see in the opposite sex or what they think the opposite sex sees in them.

What this probably means is not the ability to make jokes but the capacity to share a laugh when things go wrong. Suppose you turn out not to be as sexy or intelligent as your partner had hoped or something goes appallingly wrong in your life together. A good laugh takes the sting out of disappointment. Having a sense of humour covers a multitude of failures and eases a whole lot of pain.

The second thing that stands out is how much better women understand what men like about them than men understand what women see in their sex. Look again at our first list, of the qualities men like in women. All the way

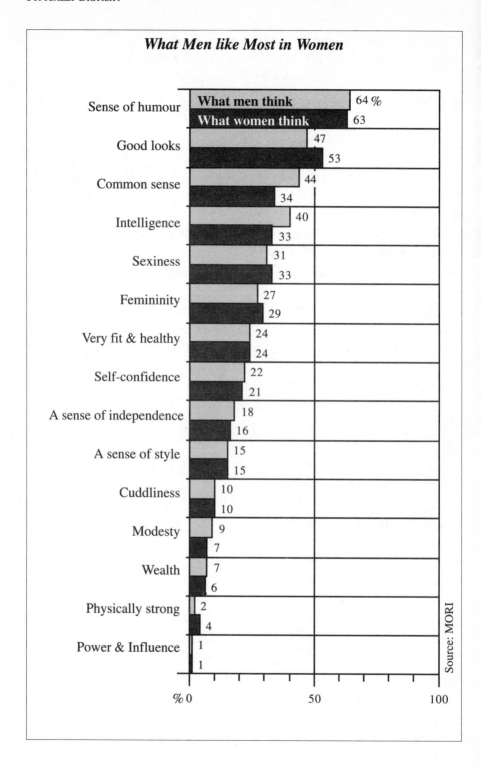

What Men like Most in Women

	What men think	What women think
Sense of humour	64 %	63
Good looks	47	53
Common sense	44	34
Intelligence	40	33
Sexiness	31	33
Femininity	27	29
Very fit & healthy	24	24
Self-confidence	22	21
A sense of independence	18	16
A sense of style	15	15
Cuddliness	10	10
Modesty	9	7
Wealth	7	6
Physically strong	2	4
Power & Influence	1	1

%0   50   100

Source: MORI

What Women Like Most in Men

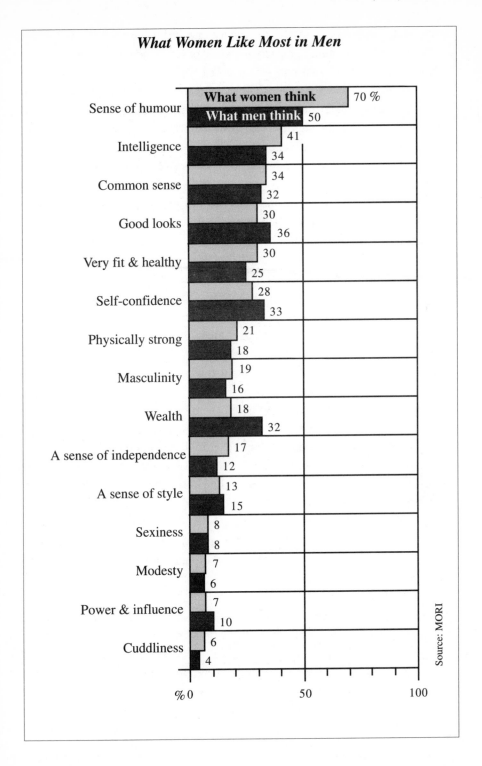

Source: MORI

down, from 'sense of humour' to 'power and influence', women rated the qualities men like in them in exactly the same order as men did themselves.

Now turn to our second list, which asked what women liked in men, and you'll see that men seriously misjudged women's feelings about them. Men began by grossly under-rating the importance of having a sense of humour, went on to over-rate the significance to women of men's good looks, wealth, and power and influence. Then they under-valued women's regard for qualities like intelligence, common sense, fitness and health, physical strength and masculinity.

Women, it seems, have got men worked out pretty well. The same, alas, cannot be said for men's understanding of them.

But women were not right about everything. Like men, they too misread the opposite sex's ideas about them in significant ways.

Women think men rate their physical attractions higher and their mental ones lower than men actually do. Our first list shows that both men and women think that 'good looks' are the second most important attraction in a woman. But more women think this than men.

Again, men and women both rate common sense and intelligence as women's third and fourth most important qualities. But more men rate them as important than do women.

Men misread women's thinking about them as well. They, too, under-rate the importance women attach to men's intelligence and common sense and they over-rate things like good looks, self-confidence and money.

What seems to be happening is that men and women both get stereotyped ideas about each other and persuade themselves to believe in a kind of caricature of the opposite sex's attitudes.

The girl who gets the man in the movies is always beautiful and the man who gets the girl is certainly better looking than the average male next door. So men and women both come to believe that looks are what count most with the opposite sex.

In fact, though, our evidence shows that the sexes rate each other on a much more down-to-earth and practical score-sheet than their opposite numbers across the sex divide are ready to believe.

But is it that simple? From what has been seen so far, a powerful impression may have been given that people would be wasting good time and money by trying to make themselves look attractive. Far better, they might begin to think, if they spent their days improving their minds in a library instead of spending time at the hairdresser improving their appearance.

Things, however, look a little different if we examine what the sexes think about each other at different ages. Then a new and perhaps a more predictable pattern emerges. Looks do matter more to the young, but as people get older the more solid qualities take over in importance.

Here, to prove the point, are the three things most often rated as important by the two sexes at different ages:

What men like most in women

What men think	*%*		*%*		*%*
15-34 *1*. sense of humour	**62**	2. good looks	**59**	*3*. sexiness	**45**
35-54 *1*. sense of humour	**65**	2. common sense	**48**	*3*. good looks	**44**
55+ *1*. sense of humour	**66**	2. common sense	**60**	*3*. intelligence	**39**

What women think men think

15-34 *1*. good looks	**67**	2. sense of humour	**63**	*3*. sexiness	**46**
35-54 *1*. sense of humour	**67**	2. good looks	**56**	*3*. femininity	**36**
55+ *1*. sense of humour	**61**	2. common sense	**46**	*3*. good looks	**37**

What women like most in men

What women think					
15-34 *1*. sense of humour	**69**	2. good looks	**46**	*3*. intelligence	**35**
35-54 *1*. sense of humour	**75**	2. intelligence	**48**	*3*. common sense	**36**
55+ *1*. sense of humour	**67**	2. intelligence	**42**	*3* = common sense & very fit & healthy	**37**

What men think women think

15-34 *1*. sense of humour	**58**	2. good looks	**44**	*3* = intelligence & wealth	**35**
35-54 *1*. sense of humour	**45**	2. Self confidence	**38**	*3*. good looks	**36**
55+ *1*. sense of humour	**44**	2. intelligence	**39**	*3*. common sense	**35**

Source: MORI

Broken down like this, something more conventional emerges. Young men do indeed value women's good looks and sexiness highly – and young women know it, even for once letting sense of humour be knocked off its perch as the most valued quality to make way for good looks.

But as the years go by the more sober virtues assert themselves. For middle-aged men common sense replaces sexiness and for the oldest age group good looks drop out altogether and intelligence fills the gap.

Women tend to cling to the idea that their appearance matters at all ages. Even the oldest group still rates good looks in its top three, though it opts for common sense as the second most important quality men look for in women.

When we come to what women think about men we find only the youngest age group mentions any physical quality at all, giving good looks second place. Otherwise, women settle for intelligence and common sense. Though the oldest women display a sombre realism when they bracket very fit and healthy with common sense as the third most valued quality in a man. That must surely be because they are all too well aware of the shadow of widowhood that looms for so many of them.

Young men, by contrast, show a depressing cynicism when they bracket 'wealth' with intelligence as the third most important quality women see in them. What makes them so sure women are after their money? They will be relieved to know that they've got it wrong. Young women are not as greedy as they suspect. They rate men's money much lower than young men think, at only ninth in importance.

Marriage

We have seen what it is that people like in the opposite sex. But what tips the balance and turns simple attraction into the commitment of marriage?

For getting married is no casual matter. It is much more than just liking someone. Get married and you take on the responsibility for another person's happiness and well-being for the rest of their life and yours – and probably for yet unborn children too.

So why do so many people take on that tremendous burden, especially today when the less binding option of living together is so easily available and so widely accepted?

In trying to discover the answer we did not attempt to lead or guide the people we spoke to. We asked them a simple question: *"What do you think are the main reasons people decide to get married these days?"* Then we collected their answers to give the results that follow.

These are the six leading reasons why people get married, that is, the reasons given us by one person in ten or more.

Reasons for marriage

- Romantics and traditionalists alike will be delighted to find that love remains overwhelmingly the primary reason why people get married. Almost twice as many people cited this as any other reason. And love's priority as a motive is consistent throughout the whole spectrum of age, class and sex.

- Proof positive of the importance of love in marriage came from those who were married themselves. They, too, put it at the top of their list – and they should know what they're talking about better than anyone.

- Widows and widowers rated companionship almost equal to love, no doubt for the sad reason that they missed just having their partners around as much as they did the intenser feelings of love itself.

- Those living together gave having children equal importance with love. Presumably they believe they are getting as much love as they need from their relationship as it is. So the most important reason for formalising it with a wedding ceremony must be children.

- Behind love, and well behind it, came companionship – love's junior relation – and having children. Men and women both rated companionship almost equally. But women rated having children notably higher. A heart-warming thought? Not necessarily. Because women also gave pregnancy as a reason for marriage more often than men did.

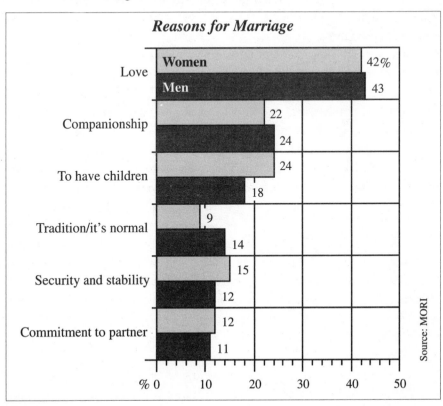

Reasons for Marriage

	Women	Men
Love	42%	43
Companionship	22	24
To have children	24	18
Tradition/it's normal	9	14
Security and stability	15	12
Commitment to partner	12	11

Source: MORI

- Apart from these reasons, no other motives for marriage were put forward by more than one person in 20. One handful cited sex. Another, pleasing their parents. Though to counter-balance them, another small group quoted getting away from their parents as a reason for marriage!
- A few others spoke of setting up home, of religion, of entering a permanent relationship so as to avoid the risk of AIDS – and even of getting married for the pleasures of a party and some wedding presents.

Marriage in Action

The world we all live in is positively saturated with tales of love and romance leading inexorably to the magical promised land of marriage. Without them there would be precious little to fill the nation's books, magazines and films. And if we only had them to tell us we might think the one interesting time in life was the phase of being single and courting.

But what about after the deed is done and the marriage has taken place? (It should be in church, by the way. Our survey showed that 41% of people still think it is better to get married there than in a register office. Only 25% disagreed, though a third (32%) were neutral on which was best, or thought one was as good as the other.)

Storytellers are altogether less forthcoming on what happens when the knot has finally been tied, when the honeymoon in the sunshine is well and truly over and the happy couple have only the rest of their lives to look forward to and nothing to put spice in it except the company of their new partners.

You might almost think that life came to a full-stop when the bride has been carried across the threshold. But of course it does not. Most people are likely to spend the longest stretch of their adult life with a husband or wife. Those years may be less heady and exciting than the years of youthful romance, but they should surely be just as interesting even if writers and film-makers ignore them.

We can immediately reassure you on one thing about marriage. Sexual love does not come to a shuddering stop when the wedding rings have been exchanged. It continues to matter a great deal. We asked our respondents how important they thought sexual love was in marriage and they answered with a massive insistence that it was very important indeed.

More than eight people in ten thought it was either very or fairly important and fewer than one in ten (7%) took the opposite view.

Assent on this went right across the board with no group expressing serious disagreement with the overall judgment. If those who were single could only guess at the importance of sexual love in marriage they can rest easy. Married people gave it just as high a rating as anybody else. But in 1991 7% said it was not important, nearly double the 4% recorded in 1982.

We will take a closer look at the ever-fascinating subject of sex later. Here, we want to explore the role of the sexes in partnership – the more down-to-earth issues of life together: who does what and who should do what.

Woman's Place – and Man's

First, let us see what people think about two old chestnuts. What truth was still left, we wondered, in those hoary statements: *"A woman's place is in the home"*; and *"Most men do not do enough to share the housework."*

This was how people responded when asked to agree or disagree that –
"A woman's place is in the home"
Men and women were broadly at one on this. Roughly one in five of both sexes still thought women should be at home while three in five did not and the rest had no views one way or the other.

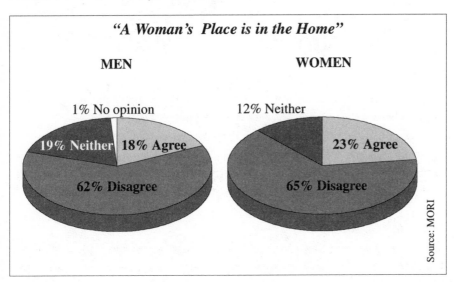

Interestingly, women had stronger opinions on both sides of the argument than men. More women than men thought they should stay at home but more women also thought the opposite. As the charts show, there were fewer women dithering among the undecideds than there were men.

The big difference, though, was not between men and women but between the generations. More than a third of those over 55 (37%) thought women should be in the home but only one in ten of those under 35 thought the same.

These differences between the generations are important, as we shall soon see.

The movement in opinion over time can be shown in another way. When the same question was asked in 1982 a third of people (35%) agreed that a woman's place was in the home. By the time of our survey, that figure had fallen to 21%.

This was the verdict on our second question –

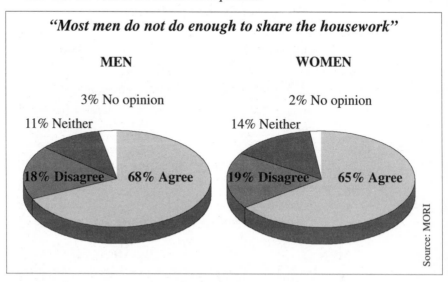

"Most men do not do enough to share the housework"

MEN

3% No opinion

11% Neither

18% Disagree   68% Agree

WOMEN

2% No opinion

14% Neither

19% Disagree   65% Agree

Source: MORI

In this case there was not a great deal of difference between young and old, perhaps because grievances over housework simmer at all ages.

Perversely, maybe, such minor differences as did get thrown up were between men and women, with women slightly less critical of men than men were of themselves and men being slightly more willing to admit they were not doing their bit than women were to blame them for slacking.

Who Does What?

We decided to move in closer on these questions of who does what in a household. For the daily routines, dull though they may seem, are the real underpinnings of every relationship.

To do this we drew up a list of household duties, then asked who usually did them: the man of the house, the woman or both equally. We brought everyone into the argument – the single and divorced as well as those married or living together – by asking people on their own how they would divide up the chores and duties if they did have a partner.

The initial picture to emerge was conventional to a high degree. Men did the repairs, earned most of the money and handled the decorating jobs while women cooked, cleaned and washed the dishes. But the full picture was more complex.

First, the findings.

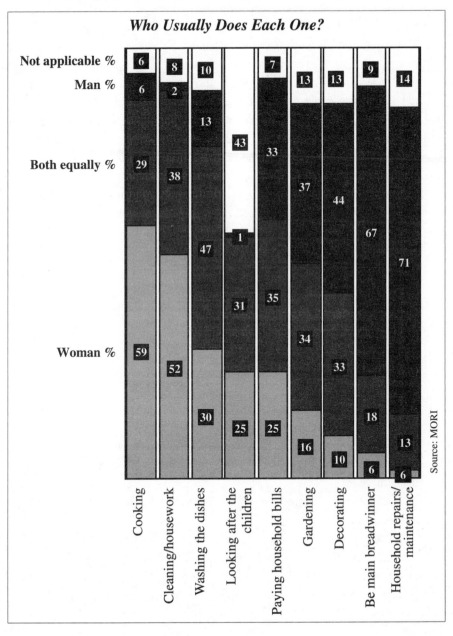

From this we can see both the conventional image of household duties – and something different lurking behind the image too.

The traditional pattern of men's work and women's is still very much in place. But alongside it has developed a far greater willingness to share jobs equally than tradition would suggest.

Only two of the jobs on our list were seen to be decisively the work of one sex – doing household repairs and being the main breadwinner, both of which are still largely seen as work for men only.

In every other case, from around one-third to a half of people said that men and women should, or already did, tackle the jobs equally.

These overall figures, however, conceal a very considerable discrepancy between the views of the two sexes about what actually happens in the real world. Men and women simply did not see the same things from their respective observation posts on the domestic front-line in the kitchen or the child's bedroom.

To reveal the extent of this gap, we now explore in greater detail how the sexes break down their respective efforts at one universal task – dish-washing.

Who washes the dishes?

	What men say	What women say	The gap	
	%	%	%	
Husbands/men	15	10	+ 5	Source: MORI
Wives/women	22	38	- 16	
Both equally	53	41	+ 12	

As this shows, a great many more women say they did this particular chore than did men, and a lot fewer women agreed that men shared the chore equally with them.

Conversely, men reported far more favourably on their own performance than women did.

We found the same discrepancy when we narrowed our gaze even further and looked at those who should know the exact truth about dish-washing from direct personal experience. They were people who were either married themselves or living with partners as though they were married.

Who washes the dishes? (Married and living together only)			
	What men say	**What women say**	**The gap**
	%	%	%
Husbands/men	19	13	+ 6
Wives/women	25	40	- 15
Both equally	50	39	+11

Source: MORI

The same disagreement runs through almost all our findings. Whatever chore was to be done, each sex felt entitled to congratulate itself for shouldering more of the burden than the other sex was inclined to believe it did.

The one notable exception was being the main breadwinner – traditionally the man's role above all others.

In this rare case, women seemed ready to give men more credit for taking it on than men wanted to be given. More women thought men were normally the breadwinner than men did (70% to 63%). Slightly more men than women (8% to 5%) thought it ought to be the other way round and women should be out earning the money, while more men than women (21% to 15%) believed the burden should be equally shared.

How do we account for these differences of perception? Were both sexes deliberately inflating their own efforts and putting down the other's? Were they lying or did they believe what they told us?

We suspect they truly believed their own stories. The man who washes up after Sunday lunch and the woman who sometimes picks up a paintbrush all too easily deceive themselves into believing that they do these chores regularly or at least share them fairly with their partners. It is more likely a question of wishful thinking than of outright lies.

But if, allowing for the erratic perceptions of both sexes, the traditional distribution of household tasks seems still to be largely in place, there are signs of real change.

First, there have been some significant movements since the 1982 survey we have already referred to. Both in cleaning and cooking there has been a 7% shift towards saying these tasks are shared equally. Similarly, 5% fewer said in 1991 that men had responsibility for repairs and maintenance and 9% fewer said men were the main breadwinners. There are also signs of a new mood among the young.

It isn't a radical or revolutionary mood we are reporting. The under-35s didn't want to overthrow the old order completely and step into each other's shoes. Young men were no more likely to take over washing the dishes or doing the housework than their fathers. If anything, they were rather less keen.

To take just one example, while 71% of the over-35s believed in the man as the main breadwinner, only 60% of under-35s believed the same.

But that does not mean that young men want to pass the job over to young women. The difference is in the willingness of the young of both genders to share out the chores and responsibilities equally between them.

The pattern was the same in every one of the jobs we listed. In each case, young people claimed to be shifting the burden – not so as to pass it across the sex divide but in order that both sexes could do their equal bit.

Youthful idealism? The triumph of inexperience? Will the old patterns reassert themselves and "men's" work stay men's and "women's" women's? Or will the youngest generation live up to its aspirations and keep on sharing out the chores in old age?

As the years go by, we intend to keep a sharp eye on developments and let you know if today's youngsters keep faith with their promises.

Divorce

Death may be the cruellest end to a marriage. But divorce is surely the saddest.

When a partner dies, the survivor suffers loss but not blame. When a marriage comes to grief in the divorce courts, though, the two partners usually suffer agonies of remorse and self-reproach.

Not a very happy subject to explore, in fact, but no account of marriage could be satisfactory if it left out completely the how and why of its breakdown. Especially since, as we have already seen, divorce is now so common an experience that one in 25 adults (4%) have been through it.

As with our inquiries into why people marry, we did not try to guide our respondents in any particular direction by suggesting reasons why people got divorced. We simply asked: *"What do you think are the main causes of divorce these days?"* Then we noted, grouped and tabulated the answers.

The first thing to strike us when we had done that was how very differently people see divorce to either marriage or attraction. You might imagine that divorce was just the flip side of all those things that attract people to each other and draw them into marriage in the first place. But that is not what people believe. We were not told that divorce happens when, say, a wife discovers that her husband doesn't after all have the intelligence, common sense and good looks which first attracted her, or when a husband finds out that his wife is not as sexy or feminine as he'd hoped.

Not one single person blamed the absence of that sought-after sense of humour for anybody's marriage falling apart.

If the story of courtship and marriage has the feel of a romance, the story of divorce is more like a back-streets melodrama: all poverty, infidelity, loneliness and sleaze.

By far the most common cause of divorce, people believe, is money – or rather the lack of it. After that comes infidelity. Then growing apart.

Here are the 10 leading reasons for divorce to emerge from our survey:

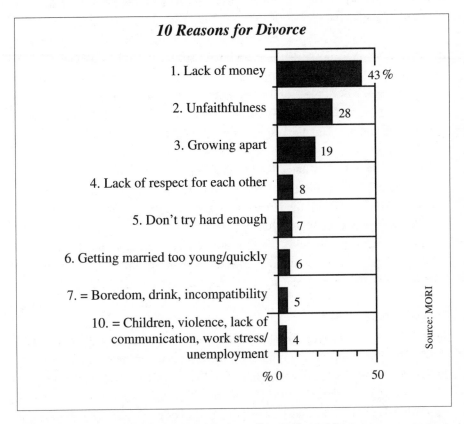

This pattern of belief about divorce is broadly confirmed by every group, most importantly by the divorced themselves, though there is some difference in the perceptions of men and women who have been divorced. Both agree that money is the biggest problem. But divorced men emphasise growing apart above unfaithfulness while women rate the two as equally important.

It is deeply sobering to realise how insignificant a part the attractions people once saw in the opposite sex play in marriages that disintegrate.

Maybe, in the high excitement of courting, people get their priorities wrong. Good looks, intelligence, sexiness and all the other ingredients of attraction matter not a hoot when marriage goes wrong (everyone is agreed that poor sex plays almost no part in divorce, including the divorced themselves).

Love, the most highly rated reason for marriage, flies out the window, taking companionship and every other reason with it. Divorce is another country.

It makes one think: is that minority of women – one in five – who values wealth in her man not the cynic men might believe but the realist? Considering how important a role lack of money plays in divorce, that minority may have the right priorities after all.

We wondered if people were disturbed enough about the ravages of divorce to want to do something about it. So we put this statement to our respondents: *"The law should be changed to make it more difficult for people to get divorced."* And we asked whether they agreed or disagreed.

The result, for adults as a whole, was very even. Forty-one per cent agreed and 42% disagreed. But there were significant differences between the sexes and the age groups.

- More women (45%) wanted the law changed to make divorce more difficult than men (37%) because, we suspect, they are generally felt to come out of the divorce courts with the worst end of the deal: the children to bring up and less money even than before.
- Many more of the over-55s (54%) wanted the law changed than did the under-35s (32%). But will the young stay with these attitudes as they grow older – or will experience teach them, too, to want change? Time will tell.

Permissive Britain?

In the 1960s, Britain was the place where anything went. It was the home of the Beatles, the Mini and the mini-skirt, the birthplace of the sexual revolution. In Britain, if anywhere, the young threw off the inhibitions of the centuries.

But things changed in the 1970s and 1980s. It wasn't so much that inhibitions returned as that priorities and lifestyles altered. Times became grimmer, more earnest. It was tougher to make a living or even get a job. The Prime Minister relished older, Victorian values. Fear of AIDS loomed like a biblical plague. The smart young weren't making it in bed any more. They were making it in the City of London.

So, in a nutshell, the story of the last three decades goes. How much truth there is in it will be argued for years. But such is the myth and myths are as persuasive as truths.

We cannot cast the spotlight of our survey back into the past, except indirectly as we shall see. But we can try to illuminate the attitudes and standards of today.

Is Britain still swinging, then, as a new millennium approaches? Or has a new Ice Age set in, a kind of global freezing of sexual liberty?

There is no one-word answer to whether Britain is or is not a permissive society. But we have some highly suggestive insights into the way things are going.

We asked people to respond to three statements which we thought would focus sexual attitudes with particular clarity and perhaps provide a benchmark that will tell us how attitudes evolve over the years ahead.

These are the statements, together with the response to them:

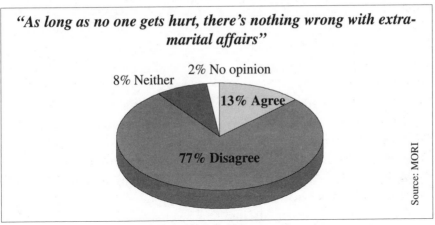

"As long as no one gets hurt, there's nothing wrong with extra-marital affairs"

8% Neither
2% No opinion
13% Agree
77% Disagree

Source: MORI

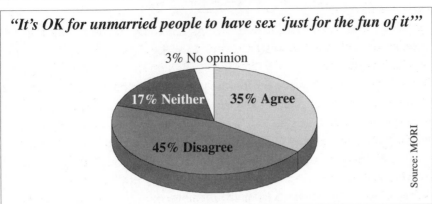

"It's OK for unmarried people to have sex 'just for the fun of it'"

3% No opinion
17% Neither
35% Agree
45% Disagree

Source: MORI

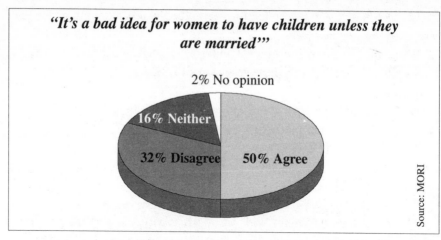

"It's a bad idea for women to have children unless they are married'"

2% No opinion

16% Neither

32% Disagree

50% Agree

Source: MORI

Hardly, you might think, an outrageously permissive picture so far. Not many people believe that even hurt-free extra-marital sex can ever be right and only one person in three endorses sex-for-fun, while half the population still thinks it is a bad idea for women to become mothers unless they have husbands.

These results could, of course, be read in precisely the opposite way. Many will think the world has been turned morally upside down when only half the population condemns women having children out of wedlock, as many as a third think recreational sex is acceptable and more than one person in ten says cheating on your husband or wife is all right so long as you don't hurt them.

But the overall response scarcely earns Britain a permissive label. Some 30 years into the sexual revolution more people still hold non-permissive views on those issues than permissive.

What's more, there are at least some signs of a counter-permissive swing. When people were asked in a 1986 survey if they thought there was nothing wrong with extra-marital affairs, 25% agreed there was not. By 1991, that figure had almost halved to 13%. Less permissive – or simply fearful of AIDS?

Let us, though, take another look at these answers, this time through the eyes of the sexes and generations.

• From seven to eight out of ten people in all groups are against extra-marital affairs. The one slight surprise here is to find the oldest age group the least critical, making this the one area of sexual activity in which they appear to be marginally less inhibited than their juniors.

As long as no one gets hurt, there's nothing wrong with extra-marital affairs"

GENDER:

Men

3% No opinion
10% Neither   16% Agree

71% Disagree

Women

2% No opinion
6% Neither   10% Agree

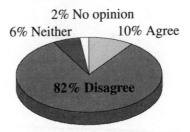

82% Disagree

AGE:

15-34

2% No opinion
8% Neither   11% Agree

79% Disagree

35-54

1% No opinion
9% Neither   13% Agree

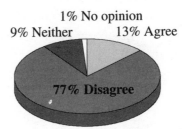

77% Disagree

55+

3% No opinion
7% Neither   15% Agree

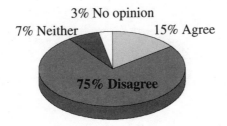

75% Disagree

Source: MORI

39

"It's OK for unmarried people to have sex 'just for the fun of it'"

GENDER:

Men

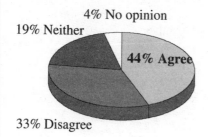

4% No opinion
19% Neither
44% Agree
33% Disagree

Women

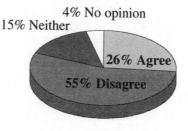

4% No opinion
15% Neither
26% Agree
55% Disagree

AGE:

15-34

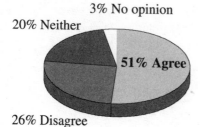

3% No opinion
20% Neither
51% Agree
26% Disagree

35-54

2% No opinion
18% Neither
32% Agree
48% Disagree

55+

6% No opinion
13% Neither
19% Agree
62% Disagree

Source: MORI

"It's a bad idea for women to have children unless they are married""

GENDER:

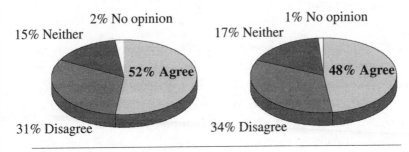

Men

2% No opinion
15% Neither
52% Agree
31% Disagree

Women

1% No opinion
17% Neither
48% Agree
34% Disagree

AGE:

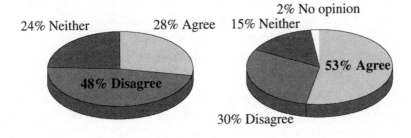

15-34

24% Neither
28% Agree
48% Disagree

35-54

2% No opinion
15% Neither
53% Agree
30% Disagree

55+

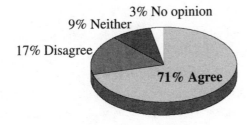

3% No opinion
9% Neither
17% Disagree
71% Agree

Source: MORI

- Women are more hostile to extra-marital sex than men and the gap between men's and women's attitudes widens to nearly 20 points when it comes to sex-for-fun.
- But the balance of opinion switches the other way over whether it is a bad idea for women to have children outside marriage. By a whisker, just over half of men think it is a bad idea, while by a matching whisker just under half of women agree with them.

Clearly, women are less keen than men on recreational sex, whether after marriage or before, but more tolerant of sex outside marriage if it results in children. Does that make men or women the more permissive?

This is a matter of definition and judgment. But, taking all our evidence together, we find the slant of women's attitudes still less permissive than men's, at any rate in the "anything goes" sense.

What seems to have changed is something different – women's attitude to having children. They are less ready to be dictated to, less and less willing to make their right to have children dependent on the availability of a husband.

If the taboo against having children outside marriage has not gone, it is slipping. And it is women who are giving it the push.

But perhaps the most fascinating differences we have uncovered are generational ones. As our figures have shown, as people grow older the less tolerant they tend to be about sexual matters.

Nothing very surprising there, you might think. It's more or less how you would expect people to change with the years.

But is it? Aren't our middle age-group, the 35s to 54s, precisely the ones who gave Britain its reputation for swinging in the 1960s? Weren't they going to change the world for all time?

Well, as they've aged, they seem to be on track to taking on the less tolerant attitudes of their elders. Their attitudes now hover in the middle, almost exactly half-way between the more permissive values of the under-35s and the less permissive values of the over-55s.

We came across something close to this question before, when we were examining attitudes to sexual equality. Then we saw in the youngest adult generation an apparently much greater enthusiasm for sharing things like household chores equally between men and women than we found in the older generations. And we wondered – would those attitudes carry over into the future?

Was it just youthful idealism or a real change in values? Would today's young men still be sharing the dish-washing with their wives 20 years on, or would they have reverted to male slothfulness?

In attitudes to sex, we seem to have come across at least part of the answer to what happens as the generations age. We have found the permissive generation going straight. It is beginning to embrace the values of the generation that preceded it. By the time the youngsters of the 1960s reach 55, they may have gone all the way.

And who is to say that today's young adults will not follow them and turn into the Colonel Blimps of the 21st century?

Some people may be tempted to take these findings with a pinch of salt arguing that, whatever else respondents to a survey may come clean about, they are not likely to tell the whole truth about their sexual attitudes.

But here is a case that might make you think the opposite. It is one in which people have revealed themselves more candidly than they might have done if they had realised how foolish it would make them look.

In the section on the **Mood of the Nation** in this survey we set out to discover what things most concerned people in Britain. One person in four named AIDS, putting it eighth from the top of a list of 24 items, well behind crime and the Health Service but well ahead of the economy or nuclear weapons as a source of concern.

We then measured the attitudes towards sex of those people who named AIDS by checking their response to our statement, *"It's OK for unmarried people to have sex 'just for the fun of it'."*

The population as a whole was against that proposition, by 45% to 35%. But, incredible though it may seem, not the people who said they were concerned about AIDS. Narrowly, they came down on the side of sex-for-fun, by 40% to 38%.

So the group of people most afraid of a killer disease turn out to be predominantly in favour of the kind of recreational sex that is most likely to give it to them.

The main characteristic of this apparently perverse group is, of course, its youth. But if you are tempted to write them off as muddle-headed dolts, take this on board first.

Our survey also shows (see **3 • The British Way of Life**) that almost one in three people (31%) are still smoking in spite of a 30-year campaign to persuade them, in the words printed on every cigarette packet they buy, that "smoking can cause lung cancer, bronchitis and other chest diseases".

One person in five over 55 is still smoking even though most of them have been exposed to that campaign for the whole of their adult lives. If they cannot give up tobacco, they are hardly in a position to mock the reluctance of youngsters to be put off the altogether more powerful drive of sex.

How Was it For You?

Now we come to the $64,000 questions, the ones we all secretly want to ask but don't often have the courage and are never quite sure if we get the right answers when we do.

How often do you do it? And how was it for you?

Sex is an intensely personal matter and we would not be surprised if people were tempted to lie about it or at least bend the truth.

Who wants to admit to sexual excess? And who, in today's sex-obsessed world, wants to admit to underperforming?

But boasting was not what we found. Our respondents were asked: *"How often do you have sexual intercourse these days?"* And they were invited to say where they stood on a scale that ran from Never to Four Times a Week or More.

Fifteen per cent declined to answer the question and another 11% said they didn't know. So, out of modesty or some other motive for discretion, a quarter of our sample excluded themselves from this part of our survey, as they had every right to do. That 26% who opted out of our survey compares with a massive 67% who did the same in 1982: evidence that, whatever else is happening to the world of sex, people are at least more willing to talk about it.

But the largest number of those who agreed to answer our questions can hardly be accused of over-stating their prowess. For they were the Nevers, a quarter of the total adult population (26%) who said they never had sexual intercourse at all.

Here, first by sex and age, is the frequency with which people said they had sex.

"How often do you have sexual intercourse these days?"
- Men claim higher rates of sexual activity than women. Nearly one woman in three said she never had sex at all, while only one man in five said the same. Male boasting? Female modesty? Perhaps. But another explanation is plausible. We return to it after the next table.

"How often do you have sexual intercourse these days?"

BY GENDER AND AGE:

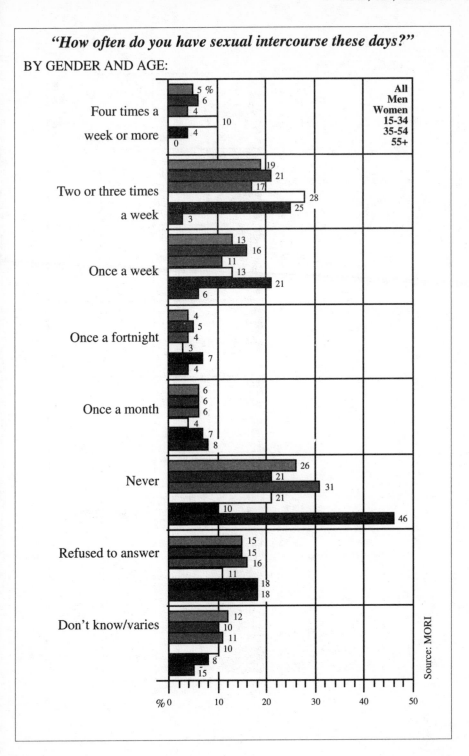

Source: MORI

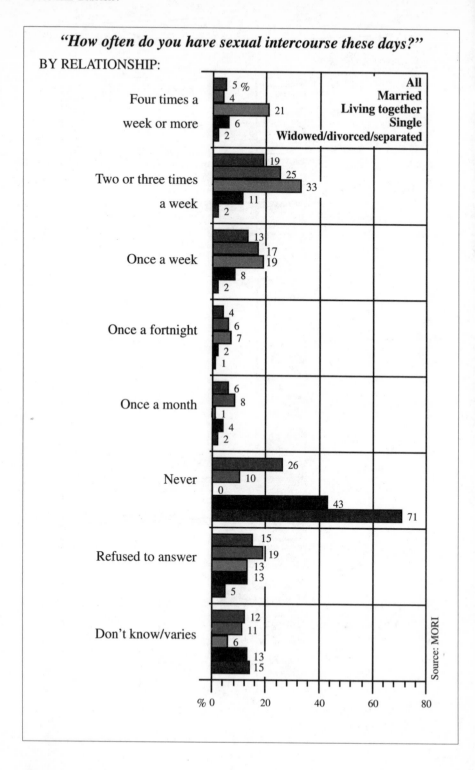

"How often do you have sexual intercourse these days?"

BY RELATIONSHIP:

All
Married
Living together
Single
Widowed/divorced/separated

Source: MORI

Four times a week or more
- 5 %
- 4
- 21
- 6
- 2

Two or three times a week
- 19
- 25
- 33
- 11
- 2

Once a week
- 13
- 17
- 19
- 8
- 2

Once a fortnight
- 4
- 6
- 7
- 2
- 1

Once a month
- 6
- 8
- 1
- 4
- 2

Never
- 26
- 10
- 0
- 43
- 71

Refused to answer
- 15
- 19
- 13
- 13
- 5

Don't know/varies
- 12
- 11
- 6
- 13
- 15

% 0   20   40   60   80

- After 55, it seems, sex peters out. Nearly half this age group said it never had sex at all and only one in five claimed to have sex on a regular, though infrequent, basis.
- The youngest who are sexually active have intercourse with the greatest frequency. More than a third of under-35s have sex two or more times a week.

But one in five under-35s said they never had sex. This should reassure those celibate young who must sometimes wonder if, by having no sex at all, they are completely out of step with their generation.

They're not. Celibacy in their age group is common. To put it another way, having no sex at all is as common among under-35s as having any sex is among the over-55s.

Now we look at the figures a different way. Not by age and sex but by marital status.

- It's obvious who has the most sex and who the least. Those living together had intercourse most often – considerably more often than married people – and the widowed, divorced and separated had it least often.
- Seven in ten of that last category never had sex. This may help explain the difference we already noticed between men's claim to have had more sex than women claimed to have.

Remember, there are far more widows than widowers. So it's probably not a question of men being more sexually active than women – or more boastful. Simply that men don't live long enough to wind up on their own without a sexual partner.

- Single people are not as sexually active as their youth and their liberated attitudes might indicate. Above four in ten of them never have sexual intercourse at all.
- Married people can take comfort. From the sexual point of view, the single years look like comparative deserts. Sexually, they are much better off as they are.

When we come to the second question – How was it for you? – we are happy to report that the response showed few complaints.

What we actually asked was: *"How satisfying would you say sexual intercourse usually is for you?"*

No fewer than 95% of those who told us they were sexually active said it was either very satisfying or fairly satisfying and only three per cent said it was not very satisfying or not satisfying at all.

- Not so much as one individual person living with someone registered any dissatisfaction.
- But one woman in 20 (5%) said she was not satisfied and around the same proportion of the over-55s (6%) said the same.
- Throughout every other category in the population, the satisfaction level was very high, coming within a point or two of 100% satisfaction all round.

Sex Change

Does it astonish you to know that one person in ten would like to change sex, most of them women? It was true in 1982 when MORI first asked the question and there has been no shift in the intervening decade.

Given the opportunity, these people would jump the gender fence and stay put on the far side.

We discovered this by asking everyone in our sample: *"If you had a choice, would you rather be a man or a woman?"*

Most people opted to stay as they were with their own sex. But no less than 18% of women said they would rather be men and three per cent of men said they would rather be women.

That is a big difference between the sexes and it suggests different motives at work in each.

But what those motives are is not clear. We are not psychologists and this is not a psychological survey, so we make no claims to plumb the depths of the gender-changers' psyche.

Nor did those of their characteristics we can measure reveal anything about them that cries out as an explanation for their choice of a different sex. The gender-changers are spread widely through all categories in the population.

The one thing we did notice was that women-who-would-be-men differ from the typical woman in being a bit worse off and a shade less happy.

Is this, perhaps, a clue? Could it mean that women who want to switch sides do not want to become sexual males, but rather believe they would get a better deal in life if that's what they were?

The evidence is inconclusive. So it is with men-who-would-be-women. They are certainly not worse off than the average. Only one thing stands out about them. They are more likely to be married than men in general.

Do Blondes Have More Fun?

It is widely believed that you can judge a person's character from the colour of their hair alone.

Redheads are supposed to be fiery and passionate. Blondes (the female variety, that is, spelt with an -e) are said to be dumb – or to have more fun – or both.

We thought we'd test out hair colour to see if it really did prove anything, so the next time you met someone new you would know if it made any sense at all to judge them by the colour of their hair.

First, we had to decide on classification. It did not seem smart to ask our researchers just to write down the colour of the hair they saw on their interviewees' heads.

Colour changes with the years. If we live long enough and don't go bald we will all end up with white manes. Besides, these days so many people's natural colour has disappeared beneath dyes and tints that simply looking at someone's hair as it is now no longer tells you much.

We therefore framed our question like this: *"What was the natural colour of your hair when you were 15?"*

From the answers, the picture we got of the natural hair colouring of the population overall can be found overleaf.

• Darkness prevailed over light. Seven out of ten British people were on the dark side of the divide (ie, from light brown to black) while only three out of ten were on the light side (ie, from fair to redhead).

This was something like what we might have guessed. Look down any High Street and you can tell the British are not a fair nation in the Scandinavian mould nor a dark one in the Mediterranean style. They're somewhere in between, a motley crew of mongrels.

More intriguing is hair colour by sex. Some colours were shared equally between the sexes but others were not. Of black-haired people, twice as many were men as women. The reverse was true of light brown. Twice as many people who said they had light brown hair were women as were men.

And there were considerably more female blondes than male blonds.

Why these differences? It could be wishful thinking. People may classify themselves as they would like to believe they looked rather than as they really did. Men, perhaps, fancying themselves a bold and dashing black and women

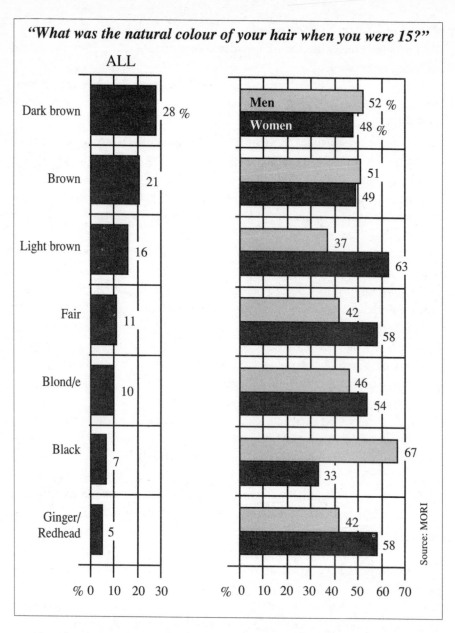

"What was the natural colour of your hair when you were 15?"

ALL

		Men	Women
Dark brown	28 %	52 %	48 %
Brown	21	51	49
Light brown	16	37	63
Fair	11	42	58
Blond/e	10	46	54
Black	7	67	33
Ginger/ Redhead	5	42	58

Source: MORI

preferring a bright, becoming light brown, blonde or redhead.

Or it could be memory. Older people might honestly forget what they used to look like. Or their memories may play tricks on them.

But unless we believe men and women have different powers of recall, that would not account for the differences between the sexes.

In fact the evidence from the generations points to something else.

When we look at hair colour by age we find that with some colours age makes no difference while with others it does.

- People who said they had light brown or black hair were just as likely to be 15 or 55+.
- But those who said they had brown or dark brown hair were a good deal more likely to be under 35 than over 55.
- While with fair or blond hair it was the other way around. More than four people in ten who claimed to be blond were over 55 and only one in three was under 35.

	TYPES	*HAIR*
	Happiest	Brown
	Unhappiest	Black
	Most neurotic	Black
	Most placid	Fair

BELIEVE IN IMPORTANCE OF
SEXUAL LOVE IN MARRIAGE

	Most	Fair
	Least	Blond(e)

SEXUAL FREQUENCY

	Most	Black
	Least	Blond(e)

CLASS

	Highest	Blond(e)
	Lowest	Redhead

MARITAL STATUS

	Most married	Dark brown/light brown
	Most living together	Redhead
	Most single/divorced/widowed/separated	Blond(e)

Source: MORI

Which raises an interesting possibility: that Britain is becoming a darker-haired nation. It could be that blondness is being bred out of Britain and darker colours taking root in the nation's scalps. That fits with what is known of the dominance of dark genes over fair.

Here is another intriguing idea about the effects of heredity.

More than four in ten of the country's blond(e)s came from Northern Britain. But isn't that where the flaxen-haired Vikings did most of their raping and pillaging?

We're sorry to say that we cannot, after all, resolve for you that burning question: do blondes have more fun?

If anything, they seem to have been having less of it. Probably because, as we have seen, blondes are older.

But we would not put too much weight on that. Hair colour does not, in fact, match up very obviously with other characteristics. The best we can do is point out a few of the more striking correspondences.

We will leave it to you to make what you like of these figures, adding only that we do not believe you would be wise to make too many instant judgments about people on the basis of their hair colour alone.

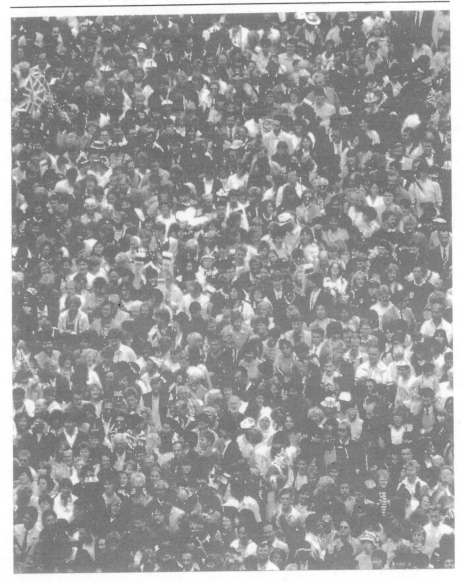

2 • HOPES, DREAMS, ACHIEVEMENTS

Most people when they're young have aspirations to achieve something or be someone.

The safest way to avoid disappointment is not to aim too high. Aspire to win the pools or become a millionaire and you are almost certain to fail (although our survey did pick up one young man who claimed to have made his million!).

Aspire to drive a car or have children, though, and you have a much better chance of succeeding.

We decided to test out people's hopes and dreams in two ways.

- By asking what, at 15, they had wanted to achieve, like learn to fly or be on television.
- Then by asking what jobs, like a train driver or a nurse, they had ambitions to be at the same age.
  (In both cases we also went on to ask which of their ambitions they had already achieved and which they still hoped to bring off sometime.)

Here is our list of things to which we thought people might aspire. We show it first in the same order we showed our respondents, then a second time in the order they ranked the list.

Get married; live with a partner without being married; have a son; have a daughter; have a son or a daughter; have two or more children of either sex; travel abroad; live abroad; speak a foreign language fluently; travel around the world; write a book; be in a cinema film; run your own business; meet a member of the Royal family; become divorced; go to university/college; be on TV; fall in love; own your own home; learn to drive; own a sports car; represent your country in a sport; go into politics; become a millionaire; marry someone you knew when you were 15; learn to fly; win the pools.

Now here is how the list was ranked, by all people and by men and women separately.

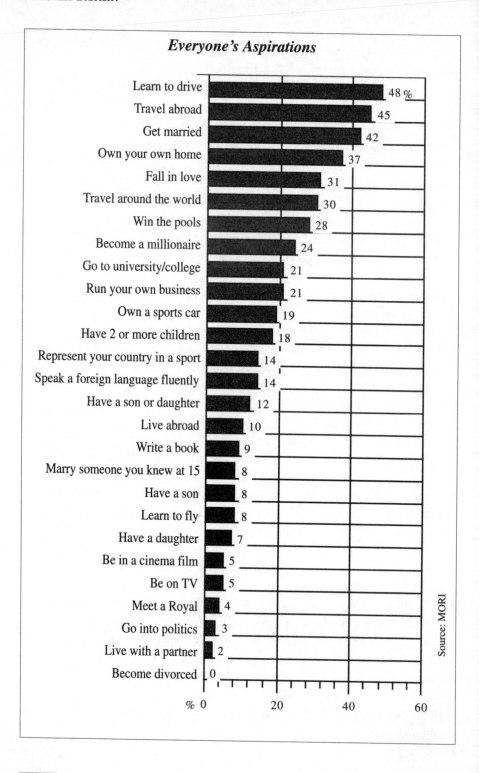

Everyone's Aspirations

Aspiration	%
Learn to drive	48 %
Travel abroad	45
Get married	42
Own your own home	37
Fall in love	31
Travel around the world	30
Win the pools	28
Become a millionaire	24
Go to university/college	21
Run your own business	21
Own a sports car	19
Have 2 or more children	18
Represent your country in a sport	14
Speak a foreign language fluently	14
Have a son or daughter	12
Live abroad	10
Write a book	9
Marry someone you knew at 15	8
Have a son	8
Learn to fly	8
Have a daughter	7
Be in a cinema film	5
Be on TV	5
Meet a Royal	4
Go into politics	3
Live with a partner	2
Become divorced	0

Source: MORI

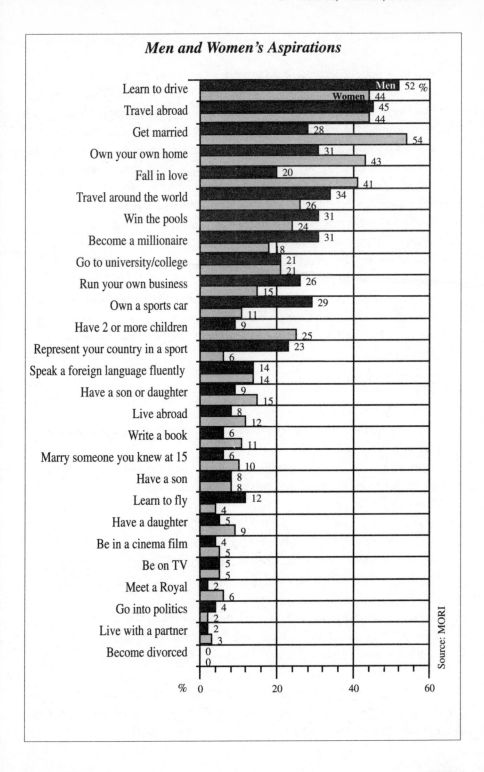

Men and Women's Aspirations

	Men	Women
Learn to drive	52 %	44
Travel abroad	45	44
Get married	28	54
Own your own home	31	43
Fall in love	20	41
Travel around the world	34	26
Win the pools	31	24
Become a millionaire	31	8
Go to university/college	21	21
Run your own business	26	15
Own a sports car	29	11
Have 2 or more children	9	25
Represent your country in a sport	23	6
Speak a foreign language fluently	14	14
Have a son or daughter	9	15
Live abroad	8	12
Write a book	6	11
Marry someone you knew at 15	6	10
Have a son	8	8
Learn to fly	12	4
Have a daughter	5	9
Be in a cinema film	4	5
Be on TV	5	5
Meet a Royal	2	6
Go into politics	4	2
Live with a partner	2	3
Become divorced	0	0

Source: MORI

What stands out from this is the modesty of people's most common ambitions.

The things people wanted to do most are the things everybody else does: learn to drive, travel abroad, get married, own their own home, fall in love.

After those first five came a small clutch of more ambitious hopes: travelling around the world, winning the pools, becoming a millionaire.

But are they so ambitious, at least as aspirations? Surely everybody has fantasised about circling the globe and making lots of money. Perhaps the oddity here is that as few as a third of people should be willing to admit it.

After those top eight, not more than one person in five aspired to any of the rest of the things on our list. Not that the rest of our list was outrageously ambitious or unattainable. More likely, the things on it were just less familiar. Not everybody's parent, aunt or uncle had done them, like they had done the top five on the list.

The sexes aspired to many of the same things. But where they did not share aspirations, they aspired very much according to sexual stereotype. Men still wanted to do what is "manly" and women to do what is "womanly".

- Men were less keen than women on personal priorities like falling in love, setting up home and having a family.
- Women's priorities were the other way round. They stressed romance and the family life.
- In "gender-neutral" areas, aspirations tended to coincide. Men and women were equally eager to travel abroad, go to college, speak a foreign language fluently and be in a film or on TV.
- Where the sexes' aspirations did not coincide they often overlapped broadly. The fact that more women wanted to own their own homes and more men to travel around the world did not mean that men did not also want to own their own homes and women to travel around the world. They did.
- The two sexes wanted the same things more than they wanted entirely different things. But it was still the case that where they differed they usually did so along sex-determined lines.

We couldn't help wondering why it was that twice as many women as men should have wanted to write a book. Perhaps it is because women, from Jane Austen to Catherine Cookson, have been conspicuously successful as writers, so women feel there are fewer barriers against their sex in authorship than other fields.

When we went on to ask how many of the things on our list people had actually achieved, the result was far from being a simple picture of success and failure.

- Some things were "achieved" by a lot more people than had aspired to them in the first place. Mostly these were things that are part of normal life, as routine as catching cold: falling in love, getting married, having children, owning a home.
- Others, we can guess, were not aspired to because until fairly recently they were way beyond the reach or experience of most people: living with a partner, learning to drive or travelling abroad.
- Yet other things might be described as unexpected and not necessarily welcome surprises, things that happen more or less by accident: getting divorced, meeting a Royal.
- In just two cases – living abroad and being on TV – achievement exactly matched aspiration. The percentage of people who aspired to each was the same as the percentage that had achieved each. Though ironically, as we shall see, aspirations were not always achieved by the same people as had originally held them.
- Not surprisingly, aspirations were less likely to be achieved the more ambitious they were. But, with exceptions like becoming a millionaire or being in a film, that still often left very large numbers of individuals achieving their aspirations.

On the face of it, then, a picture of dreadful frustration. People see either to have got more than they bargained for or less than they wanted. Mismatch between aspiration and achievement looks like the order of the day.

But there is a bright side. Twice as many people may have failed to travel around the world as had hoped to. But that still left one person in ten in the population who had made it and that adds up to a great many people – over four million Britons who have circled the globe.

And even if half the numbers who wanted one had failed to acquire the sports car of their dreams that still left an equal number who had not failed. Again, over four million happy sports car owners.

Or take the frustrated authors. One in ten people had the ambition to write a

Aspirations

	aspired %	achieved %	gap %
ASPIRATIONS OVER-ACHIEVED			
Get married	42	64	+22
Have son	8	25	+17
Have daughter	7	24	+17
Fall in love	31	47	+16
Travel abroad	45	60	+15
Have two or more children	18	31	+13
Own your own home	37	49	+12
Live with partner	2	14	+12
Learn to drive	48	57	+ 9
Become divorced	0	7	+ 7
Meet a Royal	4	8	+ 4
Go to college	21	22	+ 1
ASPIRATIONS AND ACHIEVEMENTS			
EXACTLY MATCHED			
Live abroad	10	10	0
Be on TV	5	5	0
ASPIRATIONS DISAPPOINTED			
Have a son or daughter	12	11	- 1
Marry someone you knew at 15	8	6	- 2
Go into politics	3	1	- 2
Be in film	5	1	- 4
Speak foreign language fluently	14	7	- 7
Write a book	9	2	- 7
Learn to fly	8	1	- 7
Run your own business	21	13	- 8
Own a sports car	19	10	- 9
Represent your country in sport	14	1	-13
Travel around the world	30	9	-21
Become a millionaire	24	0	-24
Win the pools	28	3	-25

Source: MORI

book and only one in 25 had achieved it. But that means 2% of the adult population of Britain have actually written a book, which adds up to around 800,000 authors.

As authors ourselves, who know only too well what a struggle writing a book can be, we are impressed at the tenacity of so many people. Although we also know that not nearly all those 800,000 manuscripts will ever be published. A lot of them are going to be gathering a lot of dust in a lot of drawers.

Achieving an ambition like authorship can be just as frustrating as failing to achieve it.

Bare figures of aspiration and achievement still don't tell the whole story. Even in cases where more people actually achieved something than wanted to, that does not mean that the achievers were the same individuals as the aspirers.

To see how aspirers and achievers match up in practice we will look in detail at two examples: falling in love and marrying someone you knew at 15. In the first example achievers outnumbered aspirers; in the second there were more aspirers than achievers.

Falling in Love

Only 31% of people said this was what they had wanted to happen to them at 15, but 47% said this was what had actually happened to them after that age.

Did Cupid's arrow, though, always hit the breast that was bared and ready for it? No. This was what happened.

- 119 men (20% of the total in our survey) and 265 women (41% of our women) told us they had aspired to fall in love at 15.
- 267 men (46%) and 311 women (48%) said they had actually fallen in love, more of both sexes than had originally wanted to.
- But only 86 of our 119 men who had wanted to fall in love were among the 267 who had done so and only 203 of our 265 women were among the 311 women who had fallen in love.
- That means 27% of our would-be Romeos had failed to fall in love and 23% of our would-be Juliets.

Cupid, it would seem, is not a very accurate shot.

Marrying Someone you Knew at 15

This was something that nearly one person in ten had wanted to do (8%) but somewhat fewer (6%) had succeeded in doing.

- In numbers, 37 of our men (6%) and 65 of our women (10%) had wanted to marry their teenage love.
- Only 27 men (5%) and 49 women (8%) had actually married someone they knew at 15.
- But only nine of our original 37 men and 26 of our women were among those who had married the person of their early dreams.

Again, Cupid's arrows had gone astray.

This particular tale, though, has a rather charming end. We also asked people which of their aspirations they had not yet achieved but still expected to sometime.

Nine people told us they were still hoping to marry someone they knew at 15. Six of the nine were under 35 and so close enough in years to make that a reasonable ambition.

But three of the nine were over 55. Which means that one person in 100 of our oldest age group was still hankering after someone they had known 40 years earlier and still expected to get them to the altar!

It's Not as Bad as You Think

If you are now feeling a bit confused over winners and losers and even a shade gloomy about ambition and achievement ever coinciding, we can offer you some reassurance at least.

The record of success is not as bad as you might think from what we've told you so far. Fewer than one person in 20 failed to score any of their ambitions and more than one in ten achieved all they had set their hearts on.

On the next page is how they scored, by sex and by age.

And if you still think that looks disappointing, do not despair. Our respondents certainly had not. They still expected to do a lot of the things on our list they had not already done.

- Men were more optimistic than women. On almost every count, fewer women expected to achieve their outstanding ambitions sometime during the rest of their lives.
- The only things about which they were as hopeful as men or more so were travelling abroad, learning to drive, marrying someone they knew at 15 and being in a film.
- The young, naturally enough, had more expectations left in them than older people. Naturally, because they had more unfulfilled aspirations to catch up with and more time left to do it.

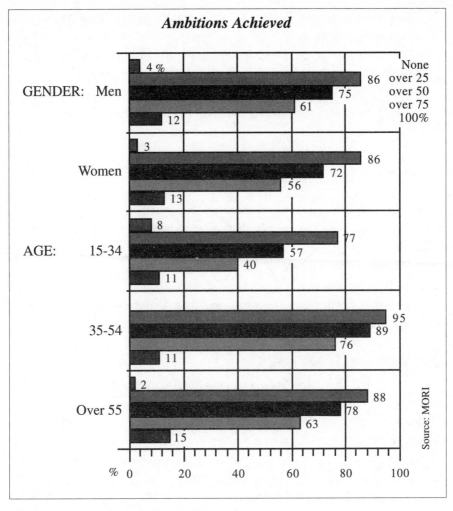

Ambitions Achieved

GENERAL: Men: 4%, 86, 75, 61, 12

None / over 25 / over 50 / over 75 / 100%

Women: 3, 86, 72, 56, 13

AGE: 15-34: 8, 77, 57, 40, 11

35-54: 95, 89, 76, 11

Over 55: 2, 88, 78, 63, 15

Source: MORI

% 0 20 40 60 80 100

- They were less hopeful than their elders only about winning the pools, speaking a foreign language fluently and writing a book.
- The over-55s were by no means lacking in ambitions. They still aspired to everything on our list with the exception of falling in love and having children.
  * Up to one in 50 were still looking to get married, live with a partner as though they were married or marry the love of their life – that hard–to-get person they knew at 15.
  * Travelling abroad was the top remaining aspiration of the over-55s. Around one in six (16%) still expected to do that for the first time and one in 25 were still aiming to make it all the way round the world.

* One in ten was full of hope for a pools win and one in 20 still expected to write that elusive book.

* Small numbers of the over-55s still harboured what we would normally think of as young people's ambitions: one per cent or more were still expecting to go to university or college, own a sports car, learn to drive, speak a foreign language fluently, learn to fly, become a millionaire and even to go into politics.

At 55, hope still thrives in the British people.

Some aspirations come later than others. We put divorce on our list, though it was probably foolish to imagine that anyone aspired to get divorced at an age when they were not yet old enough to get married.

Not a single person told us that divorce had formed one of their early dreams. But handfuls have acquired the ambition since.

In every age group, at least one per cent listed divorce among their expectations for the future.

Jobs for the Boys and Girls

Every little boy, it's said, yearns to be a train driver and every little girl a nurse like Florence Nightingale.

But these may be childish dreams which do not last beyond six. Or the dreams may endure and turn into firm ambitions.

We wanted to catch people's hopes somewhere between dream and reality, at that point in their lives when childish fantasies start to make contact with definite career choices.

That is why, as with people's aspirations, we chose 15 as the age which we would ask our respondents to cast their minds back to and tell us about their job ambitions.

Our aim was to find out what people had wanted to do in life and whether they were any more successful in achieving their career ambitions than in achieving the wider aspirations we have already described.

To investigate this we drew up a list of 23 occupations and invited people to tell us which, if any, of those things they had wanted to do at 15; which they had actually done; and which they still expected to do one day.

We also asked them to tell us about any other jobs they had fancied at 15 which were not on our list.

Here is our list, in the same alphabetical order we showed it to our respondents.

Accountant, artist, air hostess/steward, airline pilot, business manager, doctor, factory worker, fashion model, fireman, general office worker, insurance salesman, lawyer, member of the armed forces, nun/priest, nurse, policeman/woman, politician, pop star, run your own business, school teacher, secretary, stockbroker, train driver – and other.

The three jobs which were most aspired to at 15 were: running your own business (17%); being a nurse (16%) and joining the armed forces (14%).

The most popular category of all was the blank space where we asked for "other" job choices. We shall come back to them later.

Sex Bias

The same bias towards identifying jobs with one sex or the other showed up here as it did in our inquiry into aspirations. People still do opt for "men's" work if they are men and "women's" if they are women.

The clearest example is nursing. This was the second most popular choice on our list. But it achieved that status only by being wildly popular with women.

- Barely one man in 100 had wanted to be a nurse at 15. But nearly one woman in three (29%) had already decided that that was what she wanted to be.
  It was the same with other jobs that carry a marked sex label.
- One woman in five had wanted to be an air hostess, but only one man in 100 had wanted to be an air steward.
- One woman in ten saw herself as a fashion model, but only one man in 100.
- Slightly more than one woman in ten had her eyes fixed on being a secretary. But not one single man registered interest in a secretarial career. The bias was almost equally blatant with men's jobs.
- Just over one man in ten (12%) had wanted to be an airline pilot compared to only two women.
- Slightly fewer men (8%) had shared that dream of all small boys we mentioned earlier – to become a train driver. The same number (8%) had wanted to be firemen. But almost no women remembered feeling any interest in either of these jobs.

Most jobs, in fact, seem to have had a greater attraction to one sex than the other. Only being a factory worker ranked equally with men and women. And in that case the ranking was equally low for both sexes.

Just one person in 50 had wanted to be a factory worker, way below the numbers who had actually landed in that job, as we shall see.

Only with the professions like lawyer and accountant and occupations with no obvious sexual identity, like artist and pop star, did the sexes come closer to sharing the same career ambitions.

Some people may be surprised at the extent to which teaching is tagged as "women's" work. Nearly three times as many women (14%) had wanted to be teachers as had men (5%).

And people may be equally surprised at the degree of enthusiasm women showed towards joining those entrenched bastions of male domination, the armed forces and the police.

Our same list of jobs is on the opposite page, this time showing the preference of the sexes for each.

Success rate

That is what people wanted to do with their working lives. But how did things turn out in practice? As with their aspirations, not exactly as hoped for.

Over the page is the same list once more, this time presented to show, first the overall numbers of people who wanted each job; then the numbers who had actually done those jobs; and finally the numbers who still thought they would do the jobs sometime during the rest of their lives.

(Note: Blanks in this table do not necessarily mean that nobody at all was doing certain jobs or still hoping to do them, only that there were not enough to add up to one per cent. For example, five of our respondents had become train drivers and four air hostesses. But that was less than enough in each case to be statistically significant in a survey of 1230 people.)

Life, so far as job ambition is concerned, is apt to be perverse. For instance, the two jobs on our list that had been done by the most people were jobs that very few had wanted to do when they were 15.

Almost one in five of both sexes (17%) had become factory workers, though only one in 50 (2%) had wanted to. And one in ten (11% – twice as many of them women as men) had become general office workers, against the 3% of the population who had had that ambition.

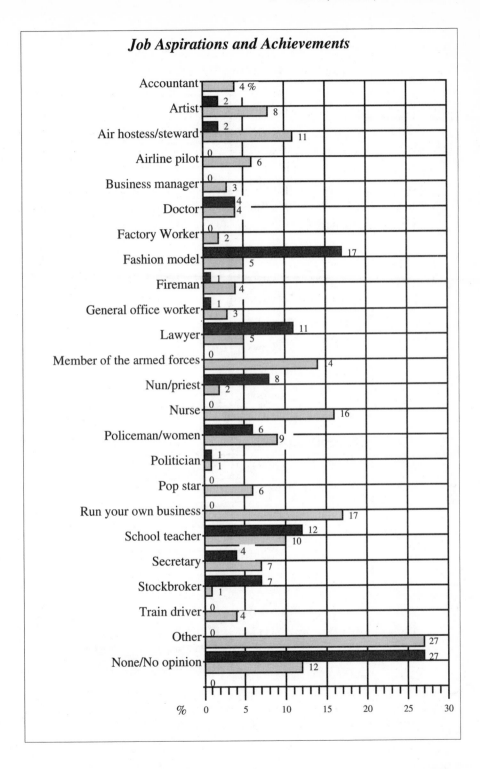

Job Aspirations and Achievements

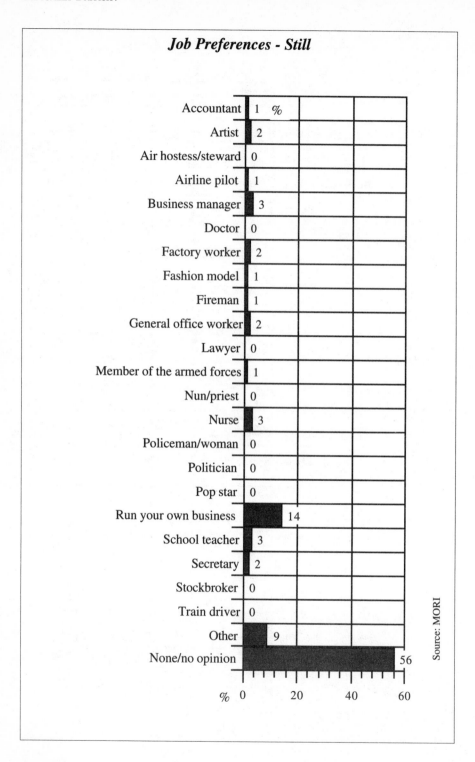

Job Preferences - Still

	%
Accountant	1
Artist	2
Air hostess/steward	0
Airline pilot	1
Business manager	3
Doctor	0
Factory worker	2
Fashion model	1
Fireman	1
General office worker	2
Lawyer	0
Member of the armed forces	1
Nun/priest	0
Nurse	3
Policeman/woman	0
Politician	0
Pop star	0
Run your own business	14
School teacher	3
Secretary	2
Stockbroker	0
Train driver	0
Other	9
None/no opinion	56

Source: MORI

As many women had become secretaries as wanted to; but they were not all of them the same people. Another example of the random mismatch between aspirations and reality.

We will now take a closer look at what our survey showed had happened to people's job aspirations in detail – beginning with secretaries.

Secretary
Eighty-six women and not a single man told us they had wanted to be secretaries at 15 and slightly more than that – 91 women – had actually become secretaries.

Just over half those women who aspired to become secretaries had got that job – 48 out of 86.

Another 27 women in our sample told us that they still expected to become secretaries. And since 20 of them were still under 35 they probably had a good chance of fulfiling their ambition. But only six of those 27 were the same women who had wanted the job when they were 15.

What had happened was that 38 women who had aspired to be secretaries had decided to do something completely different; while 53 women who had had quite different ambitions had become secretaries in their place.

But our survey actually netted 92 secretaries. The 92nd was a man. He had not wanted to be a secretary at 15, but that was what he had become.

Factory worker
Twenty-eight people, precisely 14 of each sex, told us they had wanted this job, making 2% of the total surveyed.

But nearly eight times that number – 211, or 17%, in all – had actually gone to work in factories.

Clearly, working in a factory is few people's idea of a dream job. But what about those 28 people who had wanted to do it when they were 15? How had they fared? Very well indeed. Twenty-two of them had become factory workers as they hoped – an unusually high (80%) rate of success.

Armed forces
One man in five and one woman in 14 had fancied themselves in uniform at 15. That adds up to 168 people in our survey.

A total of 103 people had joined up but only 55 of them were people who had originally wanted to – 50 men and five women.

Part of the difference was accounted for by the conscription years of the Second World War and National Service. Among the over-55s, 34 had been in the forces without ever having wanted to join.

But military service was a rare case of the oldest generation fulfiling more of its ambitions than the younger ones. Out of the 51 over-55s who had wanted to wear uniforms, 30 had done so.

Artist

Eight per cent of our sample, in roughly equal numbers men and women, had wanted to be artists at 15 and 2% told us that that is what they had become.

Can there really be close to a million people in Britain earning their livings as artists? It seems an astonishingly large number. But that is what we were told.

One characteristic about them stands out: their single-mindedness. Of the 28 people who told us they had become artists, 24 had decided that that was what they wanted to be when they were 15. Of all the occupations on our list, the artists were the ones who had chosen early and stuck closest to their choice.

The Others.

One person in four told us that they had had different ideas about their careers at 15 than anything on our list.

The range of their alternatives was wide, from chef to prison officer, from jockey to croupier.

But the range was not deep. No occupation that was not on our list attracted more than 2% interest.

The top "other" job was being a hairdresser. The four next most popular choices were: electrical engineer, vet, footballer and fitter.

Other jobs aroused hardly more than individual interest. Like the lone woman who wanted to be a gym mistress and the lone man who had set his sights on working a dustcart.

Time's Up

With the years, ambition peters out. By the time people reach 55 they are practically out of it.

But it is astonishing how buoyant some folk remain. At 55 a few people still expected to become artists or nurses, run their own businesses and join the forces.

The forces? We do not know of any armies around the world that recruit soldiers in their late 50s. That ambition, we fear, is bound to be frustrated.

3 • THE BRITISH WAY OF LIFE

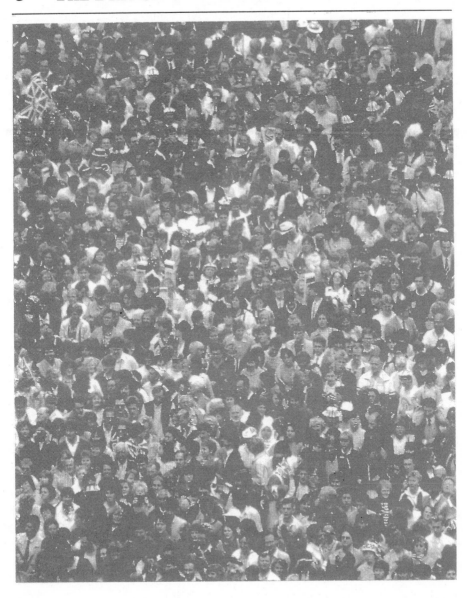

3 • THE BRITISH WAY OF LIFE

How do the typically British spend their time when they are not working? What are their priorities, their habits, their pleasures?

We set out to explore this in several ways. First, we asked people to tell us what things they had done in the previous month from a long list of activities.

The list was a mixture of the routine – like food-shopping – and the individual – like jogging. From the response to it we hoped to get a first sense of how people used their time.

Spare-time Britain

The three most commonly done things on our list were watching television or a video, going shopping for food and reading a book.

A full list of our spare time activities can be found on the following page.

We would expect television and shopping for food to be part of everybody's routine. But in an age when television is supposed to have taken over from the written word and made even conversation a thing of the past, it was less predictable that reading a book should have come third from top and having friends round fifth.

And in spite of the recession a great many people were still going out for meals and drinks. Nearly half had been to a pub and as many to a restaurant or a takeaway.

More than one person in ten had even been away on holiday in the month before they answered our question. Yet it was still only April, barely into spring, let alone the traditional holiday season.

All in all, people are getting a lot out of their spare time. But not everybody shared in those activities equally.

We will now take a closer look at who did what.

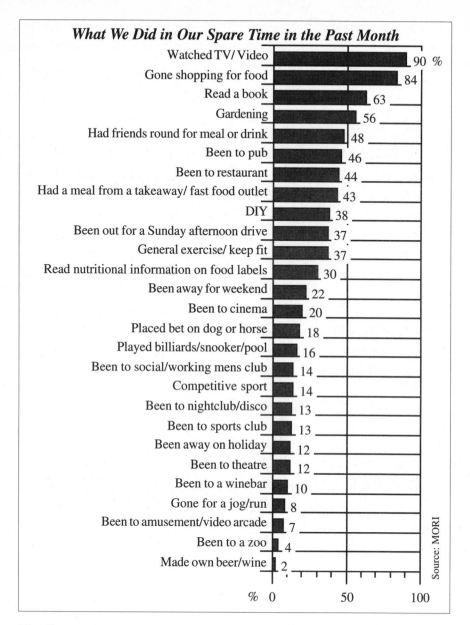

What We Did in Our Spare Time in the Past Month

Activity	%
Watched TV/ Video	90
Gone shopping for food	84
Read a book	63
Gardening	56
Had friends round for meal or drink	48
Been to pub	46
Been to restaurant	44
Had a meal from a takeaway/ fast food outlet	43
DIY	38
Been out for a Sunday afternoon drive	37
General exercise/ keep fit	37
Read nutritional information on food labels	30
Been away for weekend	22
Been to cinema	20
Placed bet on dog or horse	18
Played billiards/snooker/pool	16
Been to social/working mens club	14
Competitive sport	14
Been to nightclub/disco	13
Been to sports club	13
Been away on holiday	12
Been to theatre	12
Been to a winebar	10
Gone for a jog/run	8
Been to amusement/video arcade	7
Been to a zoo	4
Made own beer/wine	2

Source: MORI

The Sexes

If we think of many of the things on our list as treats, then men certainly get to enjoy more of them than women.

Apart from watching television, going to a cinema or a restaurant or being away on holiday, which equal numbers of both sexes had done, more men than women had participated in almost everything.

The only things more women had done than men were going out for a Sunday drive, going to the theatre, having friends round, reading a book and - you've guessed – shopping for food.

Women were certainly getting second best when it came to treats. Unless, of course, they think of many of the things on our list as for "men only" and another example of the gender divide.

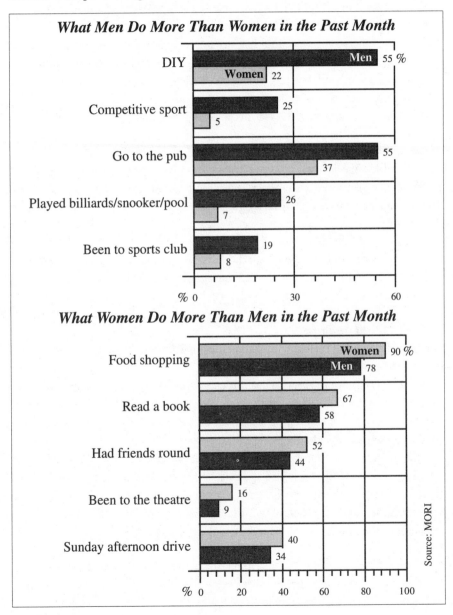

The Ages

Young people get most of the fun. Older people get left with the chores.

- More than half of those under 35 (54%) did some kind of general exercise or keep fit. And half that number had taken part in a competitive sport. But older people did not miss out completely. One in six of the over-55s took exercise or keep fit (18%) and one in 20 (5%) were still involved in competitive sport.
- If more of the young were into healthy pursuits than their elders, they were also more into the less healthy ones. Six in ten (60%) had been to a pub, around the same number (64%) had had a meal from a takeaway, one in five (19%) had been to a winebar, nearly one in three (29%) to a nightclub or disco and one in eight (13%) to an amusement arcade.

On almost every activity the under-35s scored a higher participation rate than the older age groups. The only places more of the older generations had frequented were social or working men's clubs and restaurants (52% of the 35-54s had been to a restaurant, against 43% of the under-35s and 40% of the 55+s).

- The things our middle age-group did most were much as we would expect. They did more food-shopping, DIY and gardening. And more of them had friends round and went away for the weekend.

Leisurists and Socialisers

We tried another experiment in classification by dividing people into groups we called Leisurists and Socialisers.

The Leisurists are those who did things on their own, individual pursuits like keeping fit or DIY. We defined them as people who had done ten or more of the things on our list, excluding a number of not very "leisurely" activities like food-shopping. They added up to 12% in the population.

The Socialisers are those who went in for activities that took them into other people's company, like going to the pub or having friends round. We defined the Socialisers as those who had done five or more of the following: been to winebar, pub, cinema, theatre, nightclub/disco, social/working men's club, restaurant, or had had friends round. And they totalled 9%.

- Women were much more likely to be Socialisers than they were Leisurists.
- People in the South of Britain were more likely to be Leisurists than those in the North. But when it came to Socialising, the North beat the South.

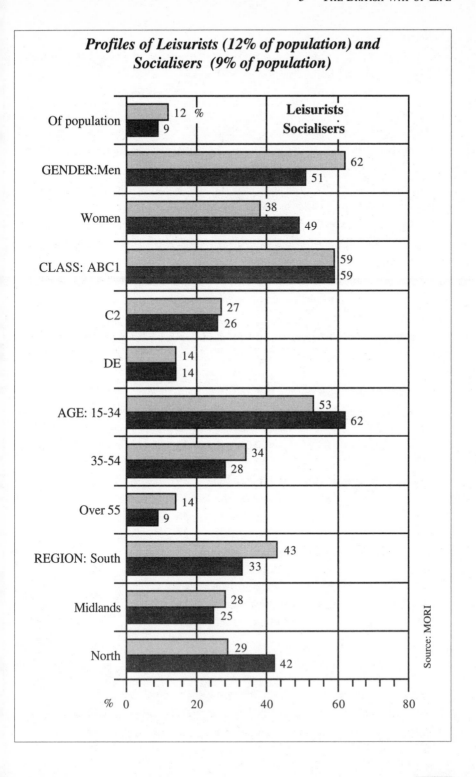

Profiles of Leisurists (12% of population) and Socialisers (9% of population)

	Leisurists	Socialisers
Of population	12 %	9
GENDER: Men	62	51
Women	38	49
CLASS: ABC1	59	59
C2	27	26
DE	14	14
AGE: 15-34	53	62
35-54	34	28
Over 55	14	9
REGION: South	43	33
Midlands	28	25
North	29	42

Source: MORI

Culture, High and Low

Everybody had done at least some of the things on that list. It would be difficult to get through life doing none of them.

Now, though, we look at a very different set of activities which represent real cultural preferences.

People must choose and make a deliberate effort to take part in them. And in revealing their individual choices to us they uncovered much of the cultural map of Britain for everyone to see.

Our list included the high arts and the not so high, the popular and the exclusive; football and ballet as well as opera and the cinema.

The results showed a rich variety in Britain's cultural life. People do manage to enjoy a lot of what's on offer. And they are not exclusive about their pleasures.

We can puncture the idea that, say, an opera buff would not be seen dead at a football match or a pop fan would never cross the threshold of a museum. Such notions just are not true.

We showed the list to our respondents and asked which of the items on it they had been to in the previous 12 months.

Here is the list in order of the popularity of each item.

	%
Library	**53**
Cinema	**44**
National Trust house/garden	**39**
Museum	**38**
Theatre	**36**
Art exhibition	**23**
Football match	**19**
Pop concert	**17**
Pantomime	**15**
Orchestral concert	**14**
Modern dance	**13**
Opera	**6**
Classical ballet	**3**

Source: MORI

- The library and the cinema were the two most popular cultural resources outside the home, as they have been for ten years – we have a broadly comparable survey for 1981 – and probably a lot longer than that.

- Football matches and pop concerts are widely regarded as the mass public entertainments of the day. But that isn't so. They came halfway down our list and fewer than one person in five had been to either.
- What are commonly regarded as much more up-market pursuits – visiting National Trust properties, or museums, theatres and art exhibitions – greatly exceeded football and pop in the breadth of their appeal.
- Pop music means popular music – the name itself is supposed to identify the music's appeal. But it turns out to be hardly more popular than classical music, at any rate as measured by people's readiness to go to concerts of each variety.

Mixing and Matching

Being a football fan does not stop people going to the opera and art lovers do not turn their backs on pop concerts. Far from it.

- *Opera* – Among opera-goers, seven in ten had also been to the theatre (74%) and a museum (73%).
  Six in ten had been to the cinema or an art exhibition (61%).
  One in four to a pop concert (27%) and one in five to a football match (20%) or a classical ballet (21%).

- *Pop Concerts* – Nearly eight in ten of those who went to a pop concert also went to the cinema (77%) and more than six in ten (64%) to a library
  One in three went to a football match and about the same number to an art exhibition.

- *Football Matches* – People who went to football matches were well above average cinemagoers and almost twice as likely as the average to go to pop concerts.
  They were even 6% above average visitors to art exhibitions.

- *Library* – Library users also took part in all the other activities on our list a good deal more than the average. For instance, 38% of the population went to museums but 52% of library users did so. Again, 23% of the whole population went to art exhibitions compared with 33% of library users. The single exception was football. Here library users were spot on the national average for attendance at 19%.

What this reveals is not simply that people are willing to mix their pleasures across all the conventional barriers that are supposed to keep apart lovers of "high" and "low" arts. It also shows that appetites for the kinds of entertainment on our list are fed by experience.

The figures for attendance are brought down by people who went to none of the things on our list. We will call them the culturally deprived. They account for one in seven of the population.

The Culturally Deprived

This group of non-attenders is not just culturally deprived but deprived in other ways too.

- Slightly more of them were women than were men – 16% against 12%, probably because ...
- A lot more of them were over 55 (25% of that age group) than under 35 (7%), so many of the deprived women were likely to be widows living on their own.
- They were of lower rather than higher social status. The culturally deprived made up 22% of DEs and 16% of C2s, but only 7% of ABC1s.
- And they had low incomes and showed other signs of relative deprivation like living in council houses and not having a job.

Cultural deprivation emerges as just one aspect of a wider state of exclusion from the good things in British life.

The Culture Vultures

These, the most eager consumers of British culture, are the opposites of the culturally deprived.

The most eager culture consumers were ballet and opera lovers. A higher proportion of them went to more of the other events on our list than any other group of enthusiasts.

Others also cast their cultural nets widely. But none matched the opera and ballet buffs in the breadth of their interests. One in five of those buffs went to nine or more of the 15 things on our list, a score unmatched by enthusiasts for other activities like football or pop concerts.

We may have destroyed another myth here – that the devotees of the "high" arts like opera, ballet, orchestral concerts and art exhibitions are the cultural snobs who would not be seen dead at any other kind of entertainment.

The opposite is the case. It is the fans of the "high" arts who show the broadest tastes. They were more likely to be seen at a football match than ever a football fan was likely to be seen at the opera.

Perhaps the real snobs are the people who would not be seen dead at the ballet.

We are What we Eat

British people do worry about their health and they care especially about what they eat. We discovered that when we put this statement to our respondents: *"Having a healthy diet is important to me."*

Support was massive. Nine out of ten – 87% – agreed and only one person in 25 openly disagreed.

Responding positively to a broad statement of good intentions is one thing. But how careful are people about their health in practice? Do they take the trouble to eat a balanced diet? Do they bother with regular, not just occasional, exercise?

To find out, we drew up a list of 17 things – healthy and otherwise – and asked people which of them they had done in the previous two days.

We chose the two-day period because, whereas in other questions with a longer timescale we were trying to find out what people did sometimes or as now-and-then recreations, here we were trying to get a picture of their day-to-day habits.

This is our list, ranked in the order of the numbers of people who told us they had done each item on it.

	%
Eaten fresh fruit	78
Eaten fresh green vegetables	77
Eaten wholemeal bread	60
Eaten high-fibre/wholemeal cereal	48
Had an alcoholic drink/beer/wine	47
Had sugar in tea/coffee	46
Had fish and chips/fry-up	33
Taken painkiller (eg, aspirin, Paracetamol)	32
Smoked cigarette/pipe/cigar	31
Drunk a glass of whole milk	30
Taken any medicine	30
Taken part in individual sport/exercise	22
Taken vitamin pills	16
Been on a diet to lose weight	14
Taken part in team sport (eg, football/cricket)	8
Taken marijuana or other drugs	1

Source: MORI

You can read a whole ferment of mixed-up minds and failed efforts to be good from that result.

- First, half or more of people tried to do the right thing by eating fresh fruit and vegetables, eating wholemeal bread and high-fibre cereal.
- Close behind these triers came a large minority who proceeded to undermine the good work by drinking alcohol, putting sugar in their hot drinks, having fry-ups and smoking.
- After them a smaller number tried to repair the damage through sport, taking pills and medicines and going on diets.
- Finally, there is the one person in 100 who ignored the whole health business and took to drugs.

These contrary attitudes run through the entire population, even those who at first sight seem the most health conscious.

We found this out when we tried labelling as Healthists those who had done five or more of these healthy things from the list: eaten fresh fruit, wholemeal bread, green vegetable, high-fibre cereal; drunk a glass of whole milk; or taken part in team or individual sport.

Clearly, anybody who had done five or more of these was at least trying to be healthy and one in five (20%) of the population earned our Healthist label. But then they went and spoiled it.

- Nearly half – 45% – had also had sugar in their hot drinks.
- Around the same number – 49% – had had an alcoholic drink.
- And one in three – 32% – had had a fry-up.

The Healthists' score on those bad habits was almost exactly the same as the national average, in spite of all their other efforts to do the right thing.

They restored their reputation somewhat by doing better than average on smoking (24% of Healthists smoked, against 31% overall) and dieting (21% Healthists, 14% overall).

But then they spoiled it all over again by being twice as likely as the rest of the population to take drugs!

Who's Really Trying?
When we take a closer look at who's doing what, we find some more strange anomalies.

Men and women are equally likely to be Healthists, but for very different reasons.

- Women consistently ate more healthy things than men did.
- Men were particularly prone to have fry-ups (40% men, 26% women). More men also smoked and drank than women.

	Smoking	Drinking	
Men %	35	59	Source: MORI
Women %	28	36	

- Men only matched women as Healthists because they were more likely to have taken part in sport, especially the competitive variety (13% men, 2% women).
- Women were more prone to take restorative action for their health than men.

Restorative Action

	Diet	Painkiller	Vitamin pills	Medicine	
Men %	9	26	13	30	Source: MORI
Women %	17	36	19	31	

- But men did practically all of the drug-taking. Two per cent of them said they had taken marijuana or some other drug, but fewer than one per cent of women made the same admission.

The young, too, seem more enthusiastic Healthists than people over 35. The bald percentages are:

Healthist	%	
15-34	26	Source: MORI
35-54	17	
55+	14	

But this is misleading. Fewer of the youngest generation actually ate each of the healthy foods on the list than did their elders – though more of them did drink milk.

Worse, they drank more alcohol than the average and more of them smoked too. And they accounted for all the drug-takers. Three in 100 of the under-35s told us they had taken marijuana or some other drug in the previous two days.

Young people were half as likely as the average to have taken any medicine and they were also less likely to have been on a diet, or taken vitamin pills or a painkiller.

The only thing that really made Healthists out of them was their participation in sport. One in three had done individual sport or exercise and one in seven had taken part in a team sport.

The oldest age group is something of a mirror image of the youngest. They were the people most likely to have eaten healthy food and least likely to have drunk alcohol or smoked.

Not surprisingly, they were the most likely to take painkillers and medicines – one person in two over 55 had had some medicine in the previous two days – and the least likely to take drugs.

What pulled them out of the Healthist category was sport. They took part in both individual and competitive sports far less than their juniors. Even so, one in ten of the over-55s said they had taken individual exercise.

All in all people's efforts to lead healthy lives seem sadly ambiguous and half-hearted. For every two steps they managed to take forward they seemed to slip at least one step back.

Perhaps the common dilemma is best summed up in the response to a statement we put: *"Smoking in public places should be banned."*

Four people in ten agreed strongly and another one in four tended to disagree. Most likely to agree were women, older people and the middle class. Only one person in four disagreed (23%). Yet one person in three (31%) smoked themselves.

So at least around 10% of people who smoked wanted a ban on their own unhealthy behaviour. In health matters, people's willpower falls woefully short of their own desire to do the right thing.

Meat or Veg?

Healthy eaters or not, the British are in no mood to sign any pledge to give up their traditional pleasure in eating meat.

Being a vegetarian or a vegan (someone who consumes no animal products whatever) may be fashionable but it is far from being popular.

We asked whether people were either of those things now or ever had been in the past. The response was –

| Vegetarian now % | 4 | Vegan now | 1 |
| in the past % | 3 | in the past | 0 |

Only one person in 25 is a vegetarian now and almost as many have tried it and given it up.

- Most of those who said they were vegetarians were under 35. 7% of this group claimed to be vegetarians at the time of asking.
- But how many will stick with their abstinence remains to be seen. Already one person in 25 in this age group had tried it and given it up.
- One woman in 20 said she was a vegetarian, nearly twice the number of men. But close to twice as many women as men had also tried it and given it up.

In their real food preferences, the British are incorrigibly traditional, though they are developing a strong taste for more exotic foods like Indian and Chinese.

We asked which kinds of food, from a list of ten, people had eaten in the previous month. Here is their answer.

Sunday roast	84	%
Fish and chips	74	
Sausages	72	
Bacon and eggs	72	
Pizza	52	
Pasta	49	
Chinese meal	45	
Hamburger	38	
Porridge	31	
Indian meal	30	

Source: MORI

Of course, this is far from an exhaustive list of foods. But the answers are powerfully suggestive.

- The stomach, it has been said, is a patriot. And so it appears from what people told us they eat.
- The grand old British Sunday roast was still tops – in spite of its high cost and claims that red meat is bad for your health.

- And not far behind came those traditional standbys – fish and chips, sausages, and bacon and eggs. Porridge turned out not to be so popular. But perhaps it has always been more worthy than liked.
- Regionally, the traditional foods were popular everywhere, though they eat more bacon and eggs in the North and more Sunday roasts in the Midlands, where nine people out of ten (89%) had had one in the previous month.
- Italian, Indian and Chinese food is more popular in the South. Around 10% more of people in that region had eaten each of these than in the other regions.

Still, these foreign intruders are making their mark everywhere. All of them, plus hamburgers, had been eaten by a third of the population.

- Women ate fewer of all the foods on our list than men, with two exceptions: porridge and Sunday roasts.
  Just 2% more women ate porridge than men. With Sunday roasts the numbers were exactly equal – 84% of both sexes.
- Half as many of those under 35 ate porridge as those over 55 – 23% to 41%.

Young people are the adventurous ones. Three times as many under-35s ate Indian meals, Chinese meals or pizzas as over- 55s; twice as many ate pasta; and almost four times as many ate hamburgers.

That does not, however, mean that young people have given up the traditional dishes. Just as many of them had eaten sausages and fish and chips as had their elders.

- Like the young, the higher social groups were far more likely to eat foreign than the lower. But with Sunday roasts and sausages there were no serious class differences.
  When it comes to what foods people eat, simply being British does more to determine tastes than any subsidiary factor like sex, class or age.

How Green?

Awareness of Green issues crops up at several points in our survey. People told us, for instance, that pollution and the environment was one of the top four things that most concerned them. And they showed their interest in a variety of other ways, like their shopping habits and their attitudes to food and nuclear power.

But how deep does concern really go? Were people willing to do anything personally about these issues? Or did they just worry about them in private and do nothing in practice?

To test this out, we put a list of activities to our respondents and asked them to tell us which of them, if any, they had done in the last year or two.

The list was a carefully chosen mixture, ranging from actions that were little more than those of an interested spectator to ones that required real personal effort and involvement.

The graph of how people responded to the list is on the following page

As one might expect, the more effort involved, the fewer people were likely to take action. All the same, participation levels were remarkably high.

- Nearly half the population had given money or helped raise it for charities with a Green flavour.
- One in three people had switched to unleaded petrol.
- One person in ten had bothered to involve themselves directly in Green affairs, from joining environmental groups to writing letters to MPs.
- One person in 25 had campaigned on a Green issue. Which means that around a million and a half people had been active in an environmental cause.

Green People

Some people are Greener than others. But who are the true Greens? We decided to label as Green Activists those who had done five or more of the things on our list (though we excluded owning a pet since that is a long-established, pre-Green habit, and using unleaded petrol because that has been heavily influenced by tax concessions).

On this basis, we can call one person in four in the population – 24% – a Green Activist.

- The more activities on the list we count in, the smaller but Greener the proportion of the population becomes.
- The Greener you are the more likely you are to be a woman, a Liberal Democrat, aged between 35 and 54, of higher social class and living in the South.
- The trend of Green Activism is upwards. We have comparable figures going back to 1988 which show a steady rise.

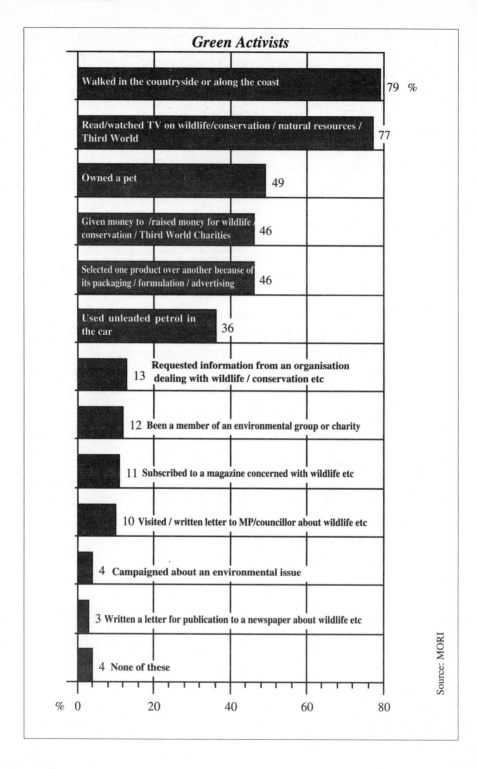

Green Activists

- Walked in the countryside or along the coast — 79 %
- Read/watched TV on wildlife/conservation / natural resources / Third World — 77
- Owned a pet — 49
- Given money to /raised money for wildlife conservation / Third World Charities — 46
- Selected one product over another because of its packaging / formulation / advertising — 46
- Used unleaded petrol in the car — 36
- Requested information from an organisation dealing with wildlife / conservation etc — 13
- Been a member of an environmental group or charity — 12
- Subscribed to a magazine concerned with wildlife etc — 11
- Visited / written letter to MP/councillor about wildlife etc — 10
- Campaigned about an environmental issue — 4
- Written a letter for publication to a newspaper about wildlife etc — 3
- None of these — 4

Source: MORI

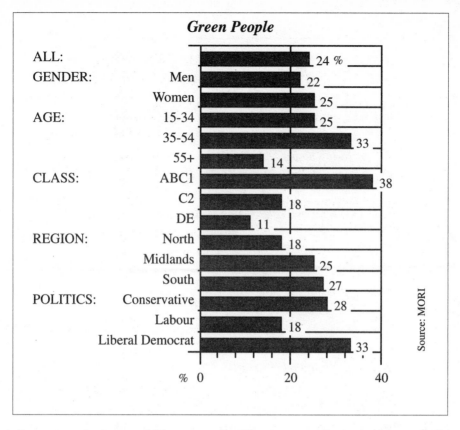

Green People

ALL:		24 %
GENDER:	Men	22
	Women	25
AGE:	15-34	25
	35-54	33
	55+	14
CLASS:	ABC1	38
	C2	18
	DE	11
REGION:	North	18
	Midlands	25
	South	27
POLITICS:	Conservative	28
	Labour	18
	Liberal Democrat	33

Source: MORI

One person in four could be counted a Green on our Green Activist scale in 1991 against only one in seven three years ago.

Who Cares Does Something

Activism is not a matter for Greens only. Many other things, as we show in the section on **The Mood of the Nation**, worry and concern the British people from crime and the Health Service to inflation and unemployment.

But who bothers? Who just worries about things and who gets out of their armchair and fights?

Not that we mean "fight" literally. This is Britain – a democracy. Here action is a question of voting, writing a letter, joining a campaign, standing for office in an election.

To find out who are the activists, the movers and shakers of British society, we showed people a list of ten things and asked them which they had done in the previous two or three years.

The result:

Voted in last election	**66**	%
Helped on fund-raising drives	**32**	
Urged someone outside my family to vote	**17**	
Urged someone to get in touch with local councillor/MP	**16**	
Presented my views to local councillor/MP	**15**	
Made a speech before an organised group	**15**	
Been elected officer of organisation or club	**13**	
Written a letter to an editor	**5**	Source: MORI
Taken an active part in a political campaign	**3**	
Stood for public office	**1**	
None of these things	**19**	

As with Green Activism, the more time-consuming and personally involving the action, the fewer people were willing to take it.

So two-thirds of people vote at elections but one in 100 stands in them.

The breadth of participation narrows rapidly as we read down our list. But that still left a lot of people pitching in.

One in three helped in fund-raising; one in seven presented their views to a local councillor or MP; the same number made a speech; and slightly fewer were elected to office in an organisation or a club.

Far from thinking that only one person in 100 standing for office shows a deplorable lack of public spirit, perhaps we should be grateful. Any more than that number could be a positive embarrassment.

As a measure of the real botherers, we labelled those who had done five or more of the things on our list as Socio-Political Activists. They numbered nearly one in ten, eight per cent of the population.

Their top five activities were: voting in an election; presenting their views to an MP or councillor; helping on fund-raising drives; urging someone to get in touch with an MP or councillor; and being elected an officer of an organisation or club.

The profile of the Socio-Political Activist is not unlike that of the Green.

There was one important difference between Green and Socio-Political Activists. Nearly everybody had done something Green. But one person in five (19%) had done nothing at all on our Socio-Political list.

These "inactivists" are predominantly young and of lower social class. But many of them have a good excuse for their poor showing. Being young, they may not have had a chance to vote at any election. No doubt many of them will join the ranks of the Socio-Political Activists when their time comes.

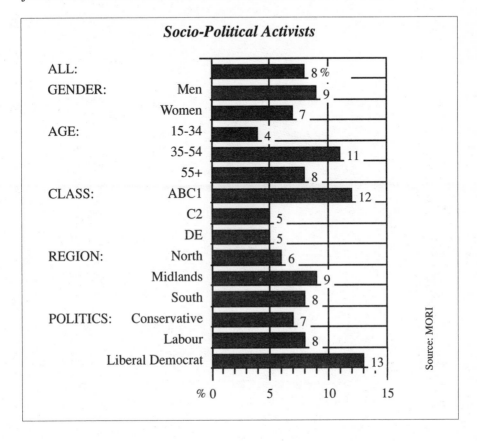

Socio-Political Activists

ALL:		8%
GENDER:	Men	9
	Women	7
AGE:	15-34	4
	35-54	11
	55+	8
CLASS:	ABC1	12
	C2	5
	DE	5
REGION:	North	6
	Midlands	9
	South	8
POLITICS:	Conservative	7
	Labour	8
	Liberal Democrat	13

% 0   5   10   15

Source: MORI

4 • The Mood of the Nation

4 • THE MOOD OF THE NATION

What is the mood of the British people at the beginning of the last decade of the 20th century?

Happy? Confident? Optimistic about the future?

Which things make them happy or unhappy? What issues concern them most? Do they worry more about their personal affairs or is it public matters that cause them the greatest anxiety?

How confident are they in their great national institutions like Parliament and the Royal family? And how optimistic do they feel about the future as they near the end of a century and the start of a new millennium?

There is no simple answer to these questions nor any single way of getting at the truth. The nation's mood cannot be judged from one reading, like the temperature of a patient in a hospital. Several readings are essential.

Our plan was to work outwards, from the personal to the general, or from individual feelings to great public concerns.

Happiness

First we looked at personal happiness, perhaps the most intimate feeling of all.

We asked a straightforward question: *"Overall, how happy or unhappy are you with your life at present?"*

The response was overwhelmingly positive. Eight people in ten said they were either very happy (29%) or fairly happy (50%); one in ten said they were neither happy nor unhappy; and a further one in ten said they were fairly unhappy (7%) or very unhappy (3%).

There was no happiness differential between the sexes. About equal numbers of men and women said they were happy and exactly equal numbers said they were unhappy.

Being happy is associated with other differences like class and money. The younger you are, for instance, and the better-off, the more likely you are to be happy.

Happy People

To show how happiness is distributed through the population, we subtracted those who told us they were unhappy from the total of those who said they were happy to get a Happiness Index for each group.

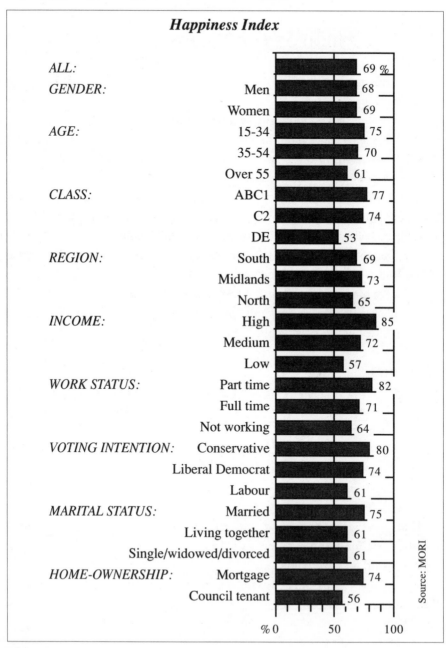

Happiness Index

ALL:		69 %
GENDER:	Men	68
	Women	69
AGE:	15-34	75
	35-54	70
	Over 55	61
CLASS:	ABC1	77
	C2	74
	DE	53
REGION:	South	69
	Midlands	73
	North	65
INCOME:	High	85
	Medium	72
	Low	57
WORK STATUS:	Part time	82
	Full time	71
	Not working	64
VOTING INTENTION:	Conservative	80
	Liberal Democrat	74
	Labour	61
MARITAL STATUS:	Married	75
	Living together	61
	Single/widowed/divorced	61
HOME-OWNERSHIP:	Mortgage	74
	Council tenant	56

Source: MORI

%0   50   100

- The happiest: You have a better chance of being happy if you are married, live in the Midlands, are buying your own home, enjoy a high income, belong to a higher social class, are under 35, have a part-time job and plan to vote Tory.
- The unhappiest: You are more likely to be unhappy if you are single or divorced, live in the North, are a council tenant, earn a low income, belong to a lower social class and plan to vote Labour.

Many things contribute to people's chances of being happy. But the biggest influence of all is money. Whether you have a high income or a low one does more to determine your chances of being happy than any other single thing.

What People Think Makes Them Happy

So far we have looked at those factors in their backgrounds which go to make people happy or unhappy.

Now we look at happiness from a different angle, this time in order to find out what people themselves believe makes them happy.

We asked which two or three items on a list were most important for people personally in determining how happy or unhappy they were.

Here is the list, as we showed it to our respondents: District you live in, education you received, your family life, health, housing conditions, job/employment of you/your family, marriage/partner, how you use your spare time, standard of living, your weight, financial investments/money.

Now here is the list again, as it was ranked in order of importance by our respondents.

	%
Health	59
Family life	41
Marriage/partner	35
Job/employment	31
Standard of living	30
Investments/money	25
District you live in	15
How use spare time	14
Weight	13
Housing conditions	9
Education	7

Source: MORI

Making comparisons with ten years earlier, which we can do from a MORI poll of 1981, we find the ingredients of happiness remarkably stable. The only major changes were that family life, while keeping its second place, had declined by 7% in importance and health, in first place, had increased by 5%.

Although as we have seen, men and women are as happy as each other overall, we now discover that very different things go to make up the happiness of each sex.

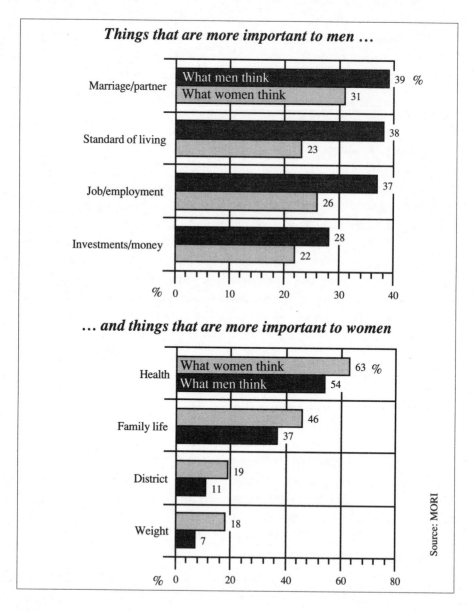

Things that are more important to men ...

Marriage/partner — What men think 39 % / What women think 31

Standard of living — 38 / 23

Job/employment — 37 / 26

Investments/money — 28 / 22

% 0 10 20 30 40

... and things that are more important to women

Health — What women think 63 % / What men think 54

Family life — 46 / 37

District — 19 / 11

Weight — 18 / 7

% 0 20 40 60 80

Source: MORI

Standard of living and weight are the things that most widely separate men's notion of happiness from women's.

- 15% more men than women rated living standards as important.
- 11% more women than men thought weight was important.

Age makes a difference too. The ingredients for happiness are not the same for the young and the old. As people get older the sources of their happiness change.

- For the 15-34s, jobs, money and education were more important.
- For the 35-54s, the most important things were family life and marriage or partner.
- For the over-55s, health was the outstandingly important priority.

We closed in further on people's ideas about happiness by asking our respondents to take another look at our list and tell us how happy they were with each item on it.

The result revealed a high degree of satisfaction with most things. Of only four items did more than one person in ten say they were fairly, very or extremely unhappy. They were weight, investments/money, job and education.

The greatest sources of happiness for the largest number of people were family life and marriage or partner.

- Only one person in 50 was unhappy with their family life and one in 25 with their partner.
- Among those who were married or living together as though they were, satisfaction was very high. Just one man in 100 expressed any degree of unhappiness with his partner, although somewhat more women – three in 100 – were, to some extent at least, unhappy with theirs.

One person in ten was unhappy with their health, which as we saw was perceived as the single most important ingredient in happiness by the population as a whole.

- One person in 25 (4%) under 35 was unhappy with their health.
- But among the over-55s the proportion rose to almost one in five (18%).

Around one person in seven (15%) was unhappy about their job. Dissatisfaction was highest among the lowest social group, the DEs, only half of whom (52%) were to any degree happy with their work.

The thing that made the most people unhappy was their weight. No fewer than one person in four was unhappy with theirs and women were much more unhappy than men.

- Exactly half of women were happy about their weight and exactly one-third were unhappy, with the remainder saying they were neither happy nor unhappy or expressing no opinion.
- Men were more content, with 65% saying they were happy with their weight and only one man in five (18%) saying he was unhappy.
- It was perhaps not surprising that when in another part of the survey we asked people if they had been on a diet in the previous two days, one person in seven (14%) said they had been: 9% of men and 17% of women.

Looking back a decade, we find people generally less happy in 1991 than in 1981 and specifically less happy with their partners/marriages (-5%), how they use their spare time (-5%) and their health (-4%).

The Future

People were far more happy with their lives now than they were unhappy. And they were also predominantly cheerful about the prospects for the future. They were less cheerful for Britain in the short term but more so for themselves in the years ahead.

Since people tend to measure their prospects in terms of the level of prosperity they can look forward to, we approached attitudes to the future by probing views on the economic outlook.

First we asked about the general economic condition of the country. Did people think it would improve, stay the same or get worse over the next 12 months?

Considering our survey was made when the main public argument about the economy was how deeply it had sunk into recession and how long it would take to recover, the response was remarkably upbeat.

By a margin of just three per cent, more people thought the situation would improve than thought it would get worse.* But there were some sharp differences

---

* This represents +3 on the Economic Optimism Index, which is the net percentage difference between those who think things will get worse and those who think they will get better. In the past, change in this index has been the best indicator of change of voting intentions in the run-up to a General Election.

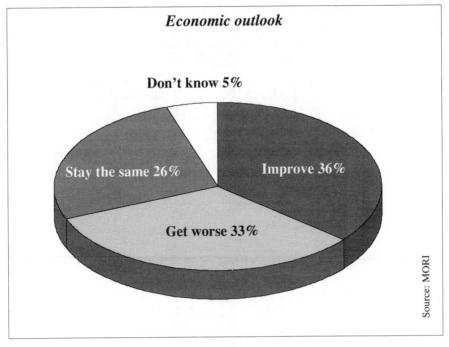

Economic outlook

Don't know 5%

Stay the same 26%

Improve 36%

Get worse 33%

Source: MORI

of opinion within this total; between men and women, for instance, and between Conservative and Labour supporters.

Experience shows that views of the economic prospect over the coming 12 months fluctuate rapidly. Any poll which records it therefore represents a snapshot of opinion at the time it was taken, and the views it reveals may look very different a few weeks later.

So next we took a shot with a longer lens by asking people to look ahead to the year 2000.

Towards the Year 2000
As people peered further into the unknown future beyond the span of a single year their optimism grew.

We asked first if they thought they were likely to be financially better off, worse off or about the same in the year 2000. Then we asked people what their reasons were for being optimistic or pessimistic.

- Almost half (45%) expected to be better off.
- Fewer than one in five (17%) expected to be worse off.
- One in four (28%) expected to be about the same.

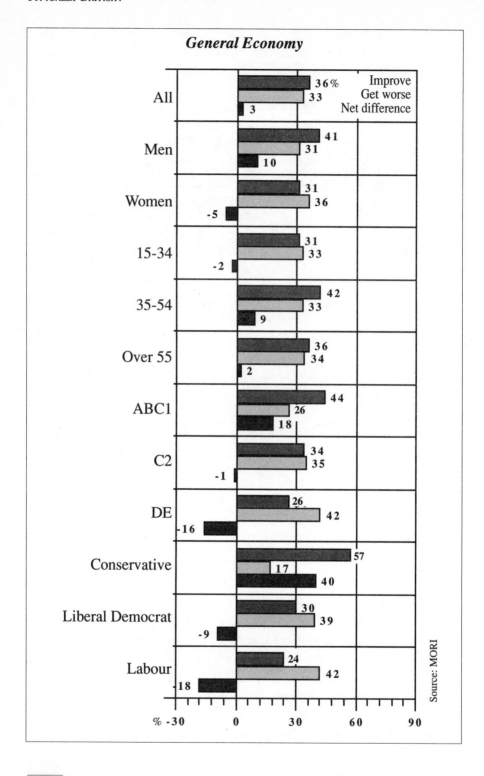

Men were more optimistic than women; the young far more so than the old; and those of higher social status than those of lower.

Here, for each of these categories, are the net figures of those who expect to be better off (ie, the total who expect to be better off, minus the total who expect to be worse off).

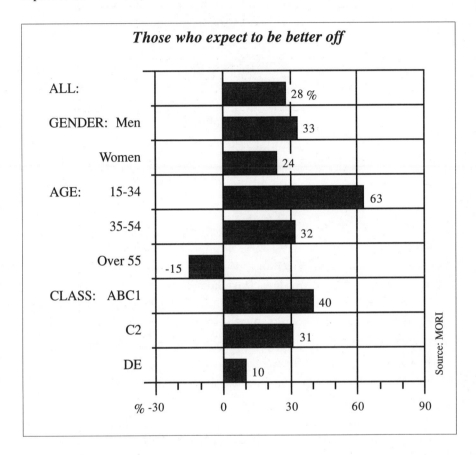

Those who expect to be better off

ALL:	28 %
GENDER: Men	33
Women	24
AGE: 15-34	63
35-54	32
Over 55	-15
CLASS: ABC1	40
C2	31
DE	10

% -30   0   30   60   90

Source: MORI

The Optimists

We then asked those who thought they would be better off what reasons they had for their optimism.

The three reasons cited by the most people were: a new job or a change of job; a general increase in pay; and promotion.

Overleaf, in more detail, are the top dozen reasons for optimism (that is, the reasons given by those who thought they were going to be better off).

Top Reasons for Optimism	
	% Mentioned by
New job	33
General increase in pay	27
Promotion	13
Savings/pension	12
Children leave home/fewer dependents	11
Paid off mortgage/loans	8
Further education/starting work	6
Improvement in economy	5
Increased value of home	4
Marriage	3
Change of government/government policy	3
Determination	3

Source: MORI

- Women, as we have seen before, were generally less optimistic about their financial prospects than men. They were more likely to pin their highest hopes for the long term on getting a new job, a pay increase and seeing their children or other dependents leave home.
- Men were more optimistic than women, especially in their hopes for an increase in pay. Trade union members in particular looked to general pay increases considerably more than did non-members – 39% trade unionists to 24% non-unionists.
- The young had their sights fixed on new jobs and promotion; 35-54-year-olds on dependents leaving home and paying off their mortgages; and the over-55s on their pensions.
- Among other reasons given for optimism about the financial future were inheritance and self-employment. 2% of people looked to each to improve their prospects. That means close to one million people were aiming to switch from paid employment to becoming their own bosses and the same number anticipated being left a substantial sum of money in somebody's will.

The Pessimists

The three reasons cited by the largest numbers of those who thought they would be worse off in the year 2000 were: that their incomes were fixed or would rise less than inflation (32%); retirement (26%); and higher general expenses (22%).

Other reasons were –

- Reduced income   17%
- Unemployment   12%
- Spending more than earning   12%

Women may have been less optimistic about becoming better off by the end of the century. But they were no more pessimistic than men that they would be worse off.

Different things worried the sexes. Men feared losing their jobs, inflation and retirement; women higher expenses and a reduced income.

Pessimism, though, was highest for the oldest. On virtually every count, a higher proportion of the over-55s believed they would be worse off.

The one thing they feared less than others was losing their jobs.

What is Happiness?

So far in this section, we have looked at how happy people are and their reasons for happiness and also at their optimism about the economic future.

Now we try the experiment of matching up the answers.

What we did was cross-tabulate the replies people gave to our question on happiness with the degree of optimism they showed as they looked forward to the year 2000.

These are two very different questions with no necessary connection between them. There is no reason why someone should not be perfectly happy in the present but utterly gloomy about the future.

But, though there need not have been a connection, it turned out that there was. People who told us they were happy now were far more inclined to take a rosy view of the future than those who said they were unhappy.

These results over the page are highly suggestive. Could it be that there are some people who take a cheerful view about everything in life and others who are equally inclined the other way? Does temperament or some other factor or set of factors permanently colour people's attitudes so that they either have their faces set in a permanent frown or in a fixed smile?

It begins to look that way. But we shall return to this intriguing question of temperament again later.

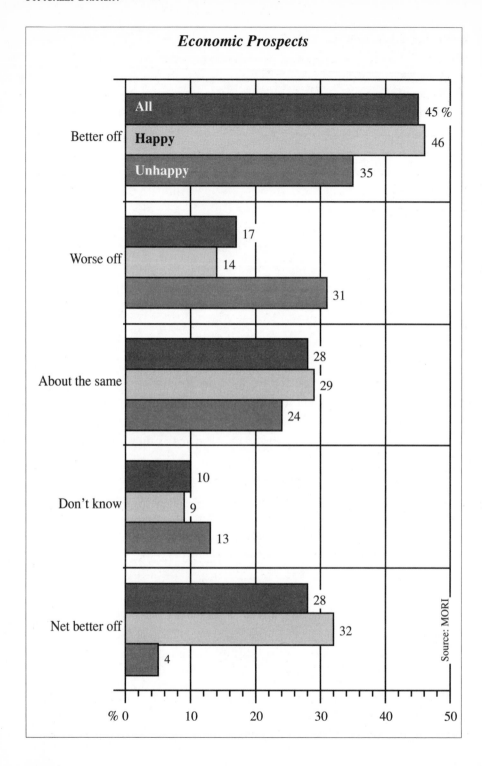

Worries and Concerns

We now widen our gaze and turn from people's personal states of mind to look at the issues which fill the nation's public agenda.

To do this we drew up a list of 24 things which we knew to be matters of broad concern and asked people to tell us which four or five things on it concerned them most.

The top three were crime, the National Health Service and unemployment.

Here is the full list, together with the percentage of people concerned about each item on it.

Issue	%
1. Crime	47
2. NHS/hospitals	46
3. Unemployment	41
4. Pollution	35
5. Education/schools	33
6. Inflation	29
7. Drug abuse	27
8. AIDS	24
9. = Poll tax	19
9. = Pensions	19
11. Housing	14
12. = Taxes	13
12. = Economy	13
12. = Nuclear war	13
15. Race/immigrants	11
16. = Nuclear power	9
16. = Northern Ireland	9
18. Morality/permissiveness	8
19. Common Market/EC	7
20. Privatisation	6
21. Value of pound/exchange rate	4
22. = UK relations with US	3
22. = Unions/strikes	3
24. Defence/foreign affairs	2

Source: MORI

Public concern does not necessarily coincide with current matters of public debate. At the time we made this survey the future of the poll tax was the political issue that dominated the headlines. But it appears here in only ninth place on our list, on an equal ranking with pensions which was not then in the least a hot issue.

There was no particular controversy about drug abuse or pollution at that time either. Yet both came well above the poll tax as matters of concern.

It isn't that concerns do not shift with the ebb and flow of controversy and events. Obviously they do. The point is that they do not always move at the same speed and in the same direction as public debate might suggest.

We can see this process at work by comparing the answers we got in this survey with the response given to the same list of issues in another survey two years earlier.

- In 1989, crime and the National Health Service were at the top of people's concerns, as they were to be again two years later.
- But by 1991 unemployment had moved up from fifth to third place while pollution and drugs had moved down from third and fourth places to fourth and seventh.
- The economy had jumped from near the bottom of the list at 18 to half-way up at 12.
- Privatisation had fallen from 12th to 20th and race/immigration from 10th to 15th.

Not only had there been a reshuffling in the order of concerns but the numbers of people who expressed concern about the issues also changed.

- Concern about unemployment jumped 15%, the biggest change of all over the two years.
- But concern about privatisation fell 11 points, from 17% to 6%, and about Northern Ireland seven points, from 16% to 9%.

This is how public concern on the top six issues of 1989 had moved over two years.

Issue	1989 %	1991 %	Change + % -
Crime	52	47	- 5
NHS	44	46	+ 2
Pollution	39	35	- 4
Drugs	33	27	- 6
Unemployment	26	41	+ 15
Schools	25	33	+ 8
Inflation	25	29	+ 4

Source: MORI

Some of these changes have a fairly obvious logic. Unemployment had risen substantially betwen the two surveys and controversy about schools and education had continued to sharpen, so it is not surprising that concern about both issues should have increased.

On the other hand there had been no obvious improvement in the crime rate or in problems of pollution that would naturally dictate a drop in concern about either of them.

But public attitudes are like that: sometimes clearcut and in tune with events and political debate, sometimes less so. There are leads and lags in people's perception of what matters and no way of predicting them.

Other points that emerge from our study of people's concerns follow.

AIDS

In both 1989 and 1991, 24% of adults said they were concerned about AIDS. But this apparent continuity concealed a significant shift in concern between the sexes.

In 1989 equal percentages of men and women were concerned about AIDS. But two years later a gap of nearly ten points had opened up between the sexes.

Only 19% of men now rated AIDS a concern against 28% of women. Presumably the surge of concern among women is related to rising awareness of AIDS as a heterosexually transmitted disease.

But that does not explain the drop in the numbers of men concerned about AIDS. Logically, more men should have been concerned than two years before.

Unions

Trade unions and strikes all but disappeared as an issue. Concern halved between the surveys to a mere 3%.

There had been another interesting change. In 1989 more union members were concerned about their own organisations than non-members. By 1991, fewer union members were concerned than non-members.

In 1991 fewer union members were concerned about inflation and prices than non-members (by 24% to 31%). But more members were concerned about unemployment (49% to 40%).

It seems reasonable to assume that people who belong to unions tend to believe their unions can protect them against rising prices but not against the sack.

Unemployment

As the numbers out of work soared in 1991, it was being said that the nature of unemployment was different this time round to all previous recessions. Now it was the higher social groups – the professionals and other white-collar workers – who had to look out for their job security, and not the blue-collar workers who had borne the brunt of past slumps.

That interpretation is not reflected in the mood of the classes thrown up by our findings. Two years earlier, in 1989, concern about unemployment had been shown by almost exactly one person in four in every social class.

By 1991, though, it was the C2s – the skilled blue-collar workers – who were showing concern in the largest numbers. The pattern looked like this:

Concerned about Unemployment	%	
ABC1s	37	Source: MORI
C2s	47	
DEs	42	

The higher social classes had in fact become relatively less concerned, in spite of all the stories that they now stood in the front line of those at risk of the dole queue.

Something else had changed too: the level of concern in different parts of the country. In 1989, far fewer people in the South had expressed concern than people in other regions. Two years later, levels of concern had shifted to wipe out those differences.

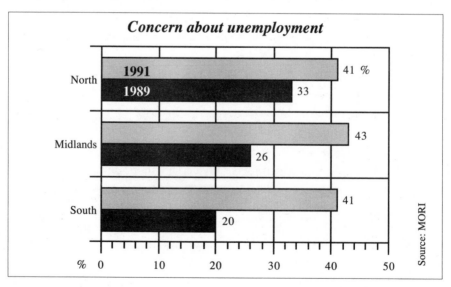

Fearfulness about jobs turned out to have shifted between classes, although unexpectedly the higher social classes were the least worried. But the biggest shift was regional. Just as many dwellers in the once prosperous South were now feeling alarm as in the old industrial regions of Britain which had so often carried the burden of fear of unemployment.

Sexes/Classes

- More women were concerned than men about: AIDS, the NHS, drug abuse, housing and nuclear weapons.
- More men than women were concerned about: the economy, inflation, taxation and jobs.
- Nearly three times as many people under 35 worried about AIDS as did those over 55.
- Five times as many over-55s were concerned about pensions and social security as under-35s.
- The major concerns of the under-35s were: AIDS, drug abuse, housing, education, nuclear war; of the 55+s: inflation, pensions, social security; of the 35-54s: crime, the economy and immigration.

Worries and Worriers

Having learned something about the range and breadth of people's concerns we will now take a look at their depth.

When people said that crime was their top concern and unemployment ran it close, that told us how many people were concerned about those and other things.

But it did not reveal how deeply feelings ran.

Did people really care about what they said concerned them? Or were they doing no more than register an awareness of matters they knew were serious or important?

To explore the depth of people's feelings, we raised a series of issues and asked how much people worried about them: a great deal, a fair amount, a little, or not at all.

Looked at like this, people's three top worries were: vandalism and crime in their areas; their own health and that of their family; and not having enough money.

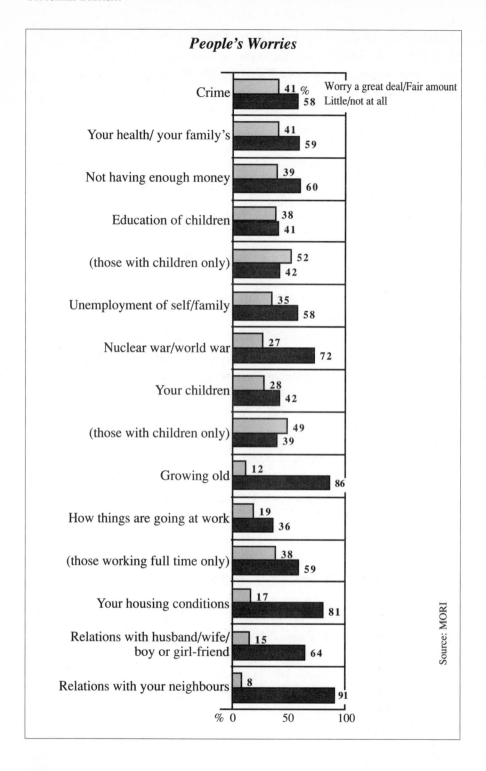

People's Worries

	Worry a great deal/Fair amount — Little/not at all
Crime	41 % / 58
Your health/ your family's	41 / 59
Not having enough money	39 / 60
Education of children	38 / 41
(those with children only)	52 / 42
Unemployment of self/family	35 / 58
Nuclear war/world war	27 / 72
Your children	28 / 42
(those with children only)	49 / 39
Growing old	12 / 86
How things are going at work	19 / 36
(those working full time only)	38 / 59
Your housing conditions	17 / 81
Relations with husband/wife/ boy or girl-friend	15 / 64
Relations with your neighbours	8 / 91

Source: MORI

Whatever else we might say about them, these results reinforce our impression that Britain is basically a cheerful nation.

Not even the top worries on the list – crime and health – worried as many as half the people. As a nation, the British worry less rather than more.

There are differences within our groups. But they are not surprising ones. The young, the DEs and council tenants worry about not having enough money; the over-55s and people without children do not worry much about the education of children; and so on. All very much as you might expect.

Far more interesting is the fact that some people worry away at a lot of things while others seem incapable of worrying much about anything at all.

Who Are the Worriers?

The spectrum of people's worries is like a steeply shelving beach. Shallow at one end, fathoms deep at the other.

At the shallow end we find a substantial minority – one person in seven or 14% – who could not bring themselves to worry about a single one of the 12 items on our list.

At the deep end we find a tiny minority of one person in 100 who worried about 11 or even all 12 items.

Clearly, some people are doing more than their fair share of worrying and others are doing less. Some carry the whole burden of the nation's worries on their shoulders; others simply shrug the whole lot off as none of their business.

To find out who the biggest worriers are and who the least we tried another experiment. We banded people together in groups according to the number of items on our list of worries they said worried them a great deal.

Those who worried a great deal about five or more items we labelled Neurotics; those who worried about three to four items we labelled Anxious; those who worried about one or two we called Relaxed; and those who worried about none at all we called Placid.

We should make it absolutely clear that these are not clinical descriptions of the type a psychologist might make. They are no more than handy labels we have slipped around the necks of groups in the population to place them on the scale of worriers.

Measured on this scale the great majority of people – around three in four – emerged as either Relaxed or Placid: further confirmation of our impression that Britain is an easy-going nation.

The remainder were either Neurotic or Anxious. Roughly one person in 12 is a Neurotic by our count.

But do these labels stand up to further testing? Or are they just a crude way of lumping together people's answers to one question?

In fact, when we double-checked them against other evidence in our survey the labels stood up unexpectedly well.

If those labels were anything like right, then we would, for instance, expect the Neurotics to be less optimistic than the Placids and less happy too. And that is precisely what we did find.

Here is how the Neurotics-to-Placids scored on our Happiness and Economic Optimism Indeces.

Happiness Index
(ie, those who said they were happy, less those who were not)

	%	
Neurotic	41	Source: MORI
Anxious	46	
Relaxed	66	
Placid	85	

Economic Optimism Index
(ie, those who think the economy will improve, less those who do not)

	%	
Neurotic	- 16	Source: MORI
Anxious	- 20	
Relaxed	+ 7	
Placid	+10	

Again and again as we search through our survey evidence we find our Neurotics and our Placids behaving according to type.

Some examples:

- Women who would rather be men were nearly three times more likely to be Neurotics than Placids.
- Neurotics were almost twice as likely be on diets as Placids.
- In response to a series of questions about the state of Britain (see **Britain in the World**) the Neurotics regularly took the gloomy view. They were –
  * Three times more likely than the Placids to agree that Britain has lost its role in the world.

* Nearly twice as ready to believe that Britain would be engaged in another war within ten years.
* The only significant group of people in which a majority said that if they had the opportunity they would emigrate.

After which it will surely come as no surprise to learn that the Neurotics were the group least sympathetic to a ban on smoking in public places.

The Worrying Classes

So who are the worriers? Who are those people who take so much of the nation's worry-burden off everybody else's shoulders?

The short answer is – they could be anybody. The worriers are scattered pretty evenly throughout the population.

Some characteristics, though, do appear more frequently among worriers than the rest of the British.

If you are one of our Neurotics you are:

• Slightly more likely to be a woman than a man – 58% of Neurotics were women, 42% men.
• Considerably more likely to be young than old – 57% of Neurotics were 15-34s, 22% 35-54s, 21% over- 55s.
• Likely to be of lower than higher social class – 41% were DEs, 28% C2s, 31% ABC1s.
• Much more likely to vote Labour than Liberal Democrat or Conservative – 48% were Labour supporters, 10% Liberal Democrat, 11% Conservative.
• More likely to be on a low income than a high – 35% were low income earners, 22% medium, 9% high.

And finally, you are much more likely to have black hair if you are a Neurotic. 7% of the population claimed to have black hair. But 18% of Neurotics did against only 3% of Placids.

Who Do We Trust?

There is more to the mood of the nation than its happiness and its optimism, its worries or concerns.

What it thinks of its major institutions is important too. It is reasonable to believe that a society will not be content if its citizens do not respect the institutions which run it and them.

Or is it reasonable? What we seem to find in Britain is that people regard the pillars of their society with a strange mixture of deference and contempt. But the picture is not simple, as we shall see.

We showed a list of people and organisations which mixed institutions like the Church and the legal system with professions like doctors and the police. Then we asked our respondents to tell us which they were satisfied with in how they were performing their role in society and which they were dissatisfied with. We subtracted those who were dissatisfied from those who were satisfied to produce a Satisfaction Index. Here it is:

Profession/ Institution	Satisfaction Index
	%
Doctors	44
Armed forces	44
Royals	17
Universities	11
Police	9
BBC	4
ITV	3
The Church	3
Teachers	- 3
Major companies	- 5
Architects	- 6
Civil service	- 8
National newspapers	- 18
Legal system	- 20
National Health Service	- 20
Trade unions	- 22
Parliament	- 31
Government Ministers	- 36

Source: MORI

Note the huge span between the top and bottom of our list. From doctors to Government Ministers there is a drop of no less than 80 points, from strongly positive approval to almost equally strong disapproval.

We have no survey with which we can make direct comparisons. But a broadly comparable one two years earlier produced much the same rank order and a similar gap from one end of the spectrum to the other.

The British appear to have a perennial respect for doctors, for people in uniforms (see the high standing of the police and the armed forces) and for the more ancient institutions in their nation like the Royal family and the Church.

They appear to have a matching lack of respect for their political leaders and the less admired professions like architecture and the law.

And these attitudes seem to survive no matter what. It is not surprising that Britain's armed forces should have been so widely admired so soon after their spectacular success in the Gulf War.

But at the time of our poll the police had been under some of its strongest criticism ever because of charges of rigged evidence in the Guildford Four case and others, while the Royal family – its youngest members, at least – had been accused of frivolity and wasting the taxpayers' money.

But neither criticism nor praise seems to make much difference. Come what may, the military, the police and the Royal family continue to be admired through thick and thin.

The same applies at the other end of the index. Whether they perform well or badly, the law, the unions and the politicians are probably always going to be at the dissatisfied end of public esteem.

When the two ends of the index clash, there is bound to be trouble. It is no wonder that Government Ministers have great difficulty reforming anything to do with the medical profession, given the great gap in public approval that stands between them and doctors.

People are certainly dissatisfied with the current condition of the NHS but the opposite is true of their view of the doctors who work in it. Reforming the NHS might please a lot of people. Meddling with the doctors would not. So if doctors dislike the reforms there is bound to be trouble.

Are the British, then, a perpetual combination of deference and irreverence, for ever bending the knee to one set of their country's institutions and cocking a snook at the others?

Perhaps. But the deference and irreverence are not evenly distributed throughout the population. People under 35, for instance, were distinctly less enamoured of the Royal family than their elders. Only one in four of them were satisfied with the performance of the Royals and almost exactly the same number were dissatisfied.

Left to the young, the Royal family would come close to a zero rating on the satisfaction scale instead of the high standing it enjoys among the nation as a whole thanks to the support of the older age groups.

This could be a sign of the start of a significant shift in thinking about the monarchy in Britain.

Some more examples of differences in satisfaction rates with people and institutions are as follows.

Sexes

More men than women were satisfied with: the civil service, major companies, the armed forces, the legal system, national newspapers, the universities, the BBC, ITV, Government ministers and the NHS.

More women than men were satisfied with: the Church, doctors, the police, the Royal family and teachers.

Ages

The middle age group, between 35 and 54, were the least likely to be satisfied with any institution or profession. The only ones with which more expressed satisfaction than older or younger people were the police and Parliament.

The preferences of the over-55s were for the Church, doctors, the Royal family and the NHS.

More of the youngest were satisfied with major companies, teachers, the legal system, national newspapers, universities, ITV and architects.

Politics

The low esteem in which Parliament and Government ministers were held may not be quite so damning an indictment of our governing institutions as it looks.

For there was a great deal of political bias in people's judgments. With a Conservative Government in power Conservative supporters were far more likely to be satisfied with Government ministers, and Labour and Liberal Democrat supporters far more likely to be dissatisfied.

Furthermore, their dissatisfaction with the Government spills over into dissatisfaction with Parliament.

Supporters of the Opposition parties were more than twice as dissatisfied with both Parliament and Government ministers than were supporters of the Government itself. No doubt these attitudes would be smartly reversed with a change in the political complexion of the Government itself.

Lack of satisfaction with Ministers and Parliament should probably be seen more as a measure of people's dissatisfaction with the Government of the day than of their disapproval of Britain's governing institutions as such.

However, confidence could be on the slide long-term. MORI's recent State of the Nation survey for the Rowntree Reform Trust updated a survey for the Crowther-Hunt Commission in 1973. Nearly two decades ago almost half the

British said they were satisfied with the system governing Britain. By 1991, only a third said they were satisfied, a drop of 15 percentage points in only 15 years.

On the Move

British people are scattered all round the world. From Paris to Sydney, from Montreal to Bombay, there are few places without its British colony, large or small, and there must be few Britons who cannot claim at least a long-lost cousin in some faraway country.

But how mobile are they in their own country? Does the typical Briton move around in search of work or a better home or a different lifestyle? And are the ones who stay put more or less miserable than the ones who move around?

To find out, we asked people: *"Have you always lived within about ten miles of here, or have you ever lived somewhere else?"*

The answer was very close to even. Just over half (51%) said they had lived somewhere else, while just under half (48%) said they had always lived within about ten miles. The remainder (1%) did not know.

This result looks more startling if we turn it into figures. For it means that more than 20 million adults have moved from one part of the country to another sometime during their lives. Britain is in the throes of a ceaseless process of internal migration.

So who moves and who stays still? Men moved slightly more than women, Southerners more than Northerners and the middle age-group more than the younger or older.

- Large numbers of people in all sections of society moved from their childhood homes to settle elsewhere at some point in their lives.
- Moving seems to be on the increase. More of the 35-54s had moved than either their elders or their juniors. It is reasonable to suppose that older people have not had the opportunity to move and are unlikely to start now, while many younger people have not yet had the chance. The apparently greater mobility of the middle group looks like a trend which today's young will continue in their turn.
- People from the higher social and income groups are far the most likely to have moved around the country. Physical mobility and status are strongly linked.

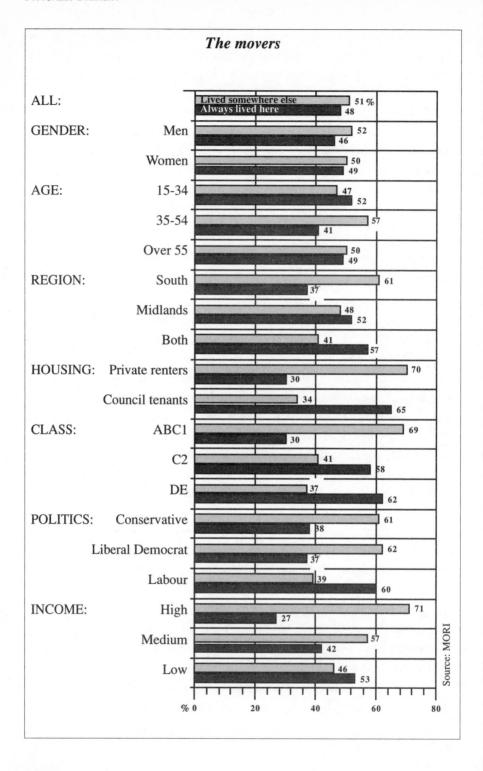

The movers

ALL:

GENDER: Men / Women

AGE: 15-34 / 35-54 / Over 55

REGION: South / Midlands / Both

HOUSING: Private renters / Council tenants

CLASS: ABC1 / C2 / DE

POLITICS: Conservative / Liberal Democrat / Labour

INCOME: High / Medium / Low

Lived somewhere else — 51 %
Always lived here — 48

Source: MORI

Late in life, people often get nostalgic for the place of their birth. If only they had stayed close to their roots instead of moving away, would they not have been much happier? The answer is – no. Those who moved had at least a marginally better chance of happiness than those who had not.

Of people who told us they were very happy, 45% had always lived within ten miles but 53% had moved elsewhere. Of those who said they were unhappy, 51% had stayed put and 48% had moved.

You are also less likely to be a Neurotic if you have moved. Of our Neurotics 55% had stayed close to home; 44% had lived somewhere else.

There seems to be less joy in sticking to your roots than popular belief would have it.

Classless Britain?

Mobility, we have just seen, goes with status and class. But are we still a class-ridden society?

When he became Prime Minister, John Major made it clear that ridding Britain of its class distinctions was one of his prime aims. He wanted a Britain where merit, not birth, was what counted.

But to judge by the evidence of our poll, there is a very long way indeed to go before Mr Major's ambitions are achieved. The British people fervently believe that class divisions still rule.

Opinion on this issue is particularly significant. There is no exact or agreed science for ranking people according to class. Political thinkers, sociologists and the opinion research industry all have their own systems.

So do ordinary people. Every man and woman in the street might agree that a Duke is a member of the upper classes. The problem with that is that any such class, however defined, would be too small to matter. It simply would not have enough members to show up in an opinion poll. Which is why opinion researchers like MORI ignore it.

But if people we think we can place with confidence on the class scale – like Dukes – turn out not to fit, how do we place everybody else?

How do nurses rate against doctors? Or civil servants against vicars? Or a millionaire against, say, an unemployed physicist? Or the captain of an ocean liner against the master of a tug?

In the end, people make up their own minds. More than most things, class is what people believe it to be.

But however slippery and elusive the concept of class may be, there is no doubt that the idea of its existence has a powerful grip on the British imagination.

We asked people to tell us whether they agreed or disagreed with this statement: *"Britain is now a classless society."*

Overwhelmingly, the answer was that people did not agree.

- Only three people in 100 strongly agreed and a further one person in ten tended to agree. But 75% disagreed and more than one person in three (37%) strongly disagreed.
- Women were a little more likely to believe that Britain is classless than were men. So were the young and older age groups. The 35s-54s were more likely to disagree.
- Strangely, perhaps, those at the lower end of the social scale (as defined by the research industry, that is) and those with less money were more likely to believe that Britain is classless than those at the upper end of the scale or with more money.

You might expect people at the raw end of a class system to see it most clearly. But that is not so.

For example, 20% of DEs agreed that Britain is now a classless society, but only 7% of ABC1s. And 17% of those on the lowest incomes thought Britain classless against only 2% of those on the highest incomes.

And supporters of Mr Major's own Conservative Party were a good deal less likely to think of their country as classless than were their Labour opponents: 10% against 17%.

Does this mean that the higher groups were realists and the lower groups dreamers?

We will leave that for you to decide. As we said, class more than most things is what you want to believe it is.

Who the British Like Most

We end this section on the mood of the British by looking at it from an odd angle. Some might say perverse. But odd angles can be highly revealing.

Britain has long had a reputation as a nation of animal lovers, a reputation borne out by one of our findings which showed that almost exactly half of British adults (49%) owned a pet.

How fond of their pets are they, though? More fond of them than of their wives and husbands, their children or their parents?

Surely not. But, incredible though it may seem, that is what the British think about each other. They actually believe that people like their pets more than their relations.

That was what we found when we asked whether people agreed or disagreed with this statement: *"The British like their pets more than their relatives."*

Nearly half agreed (46%) and only one person in four disagreed (24%) while the rest (30%) offered no opinion.

Women were slightly less likely to take this view than men (45% of women agreed and 48% of men) and the young less than the older age groups (39% of under-35s agreed; 55% of the 35-54s; 47% of the 55+s).

But agreement that the British like their pets more than their relatives was widespread, never falling below four people in ten and in every group always considerably outnumbering those who disagreed.

Among Unhappy and Anxious people agreement was particularly strong, being expressed by more than half of each group (54% and 59% respectively).

As with the question of class, we will leave you to make of this astonishing finding what you will!

5 • BRITAIN IN THE WORLD

The British are unsure about the safety of the world or their place and role in it.

But as the European Community rapidly takes shape they are more and more convinced that Europe is where their destiny lies, although they are none too certain that the Community's influence is always for the best or that its powers should be increased.

To judge by their familiarity with other countries, though, the British may well feel entitled to think of the whole world as their oyster.

We first look at the response to four wide-ranging statements aimed at testing people's general feelings about their country.

The first statement was: *"Britain has lost its role in the world."*

- Nearly half of people – 48% – either agreed strongly or tended to agree.
- One-third – 33% – took the opposite view.
- The rest – 19% – offered no opinion.

When the same question was put in a survey two years earlier the response was slightly more negative. 2% more agreed with the statement and 6% fewer disagreed, a "swing" of 4%; four people in 100 were less likely to think Britain had lost its role in the world than thought so in 1989. Britain's recent success in the Gulf War may have boosted some people's confidence in the interval.

There was no major difference between men and women on this issue. Other differences are more interesting.

Young people were evidently less concerned than older people about Britain's role. But the over-55s remember the now-vanished Empire which the young never knew.

Do working class people hanker after the Empire too? Perhaps. But it is just as likely that, more of them being Labour supporters, they took a gloomy view of Britain's place in the world under a Conservative Government.

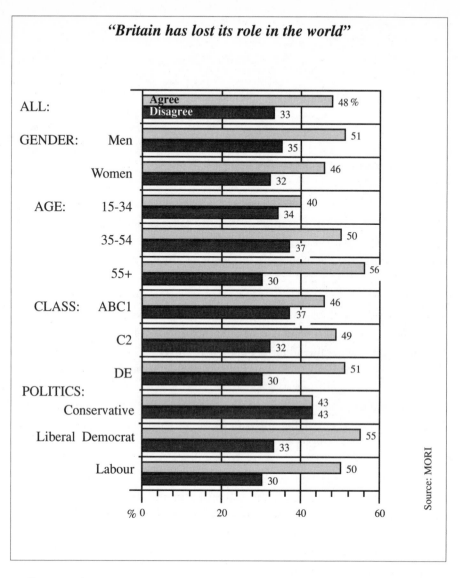

"Britain has lost its role in the world"

	Agree	Disagree
ALL:	48%	33
GENDER: Men	51	35
Women	46	32
AGE: 15-34	40	34
35-54	50	37
55+	56	30
CLASS: ABC1	46	37
C2	49	32
DE	51	30
POLITICS: Conservative	43	43
Liberal Democrat	55	33
Labour	50	30

Source: MORI

Conservatives, conversely, were more sanguine. It may be that, age aside, political attitudes do more than anything else to colour people's views about Britain's role.

Our second statement was: *"Britain should keep its nuclear weapons even if other countries get rid of theirs."*

- More than one person in three – 39% – agreed.
- But nearly half – 47% – disagreed.

Agreement with this proposition had increased significantly over two years since the question had last been asked. 9% more people agreed and 6% fewer disagreed than the last time. Again, the closeness of the Gulf War and the threat of Third World dictators like Saddam Hussein developing their own nuclear arsenals may have influenced people to favour keeping Britain strong.

On this question, too, age and politics produced the biggest differences.

- Nearly twice as many under-35s thought Britain should not keep its nuclear weapons as thought it should: 28% against 55%
- With the over-55s the position was reversed; 47% thought Britain should keep its nuclear weapons against 39% who thought not.

The political breakdown was:

Britain should keep its nuclear weapons...?			
	Agree %	Disagree %	Source: MORI
Conservatives	51	36	
Labour	35	54	
Liberal Democrats	33	54	

Did Conservatives want to keep the bomb because they believe it is safe in the hands of their Government? And did supporters of the Opposition parties want to get rid of the bomb because they believed the opposite?

Only a change of Government will tell.

The third statement was: *"I expect Britain to be engaged in another war within the next ten years."*

More people expect a war than don't; 39% agreed with the statement while 35% disagreed and 27% offered no opinion.

Once more, the Gulf may have influenced people's thinking, though we have no comparable result from two years earlier to show how attitudes might have changed.

With this question, though, there were even wider differences between groups than with our other statements.

- The sort of person who most expects a war is young, male, blue-collar, living in the Midlands, on a high income, who is a Labour supporter and both unhappy and neurotic.
- The sort of person who least expects a war is his opposite number: over 55, a woman, of higher class, living in the North, on a medium or low income who is very happy and placid and a Conservative supporter.

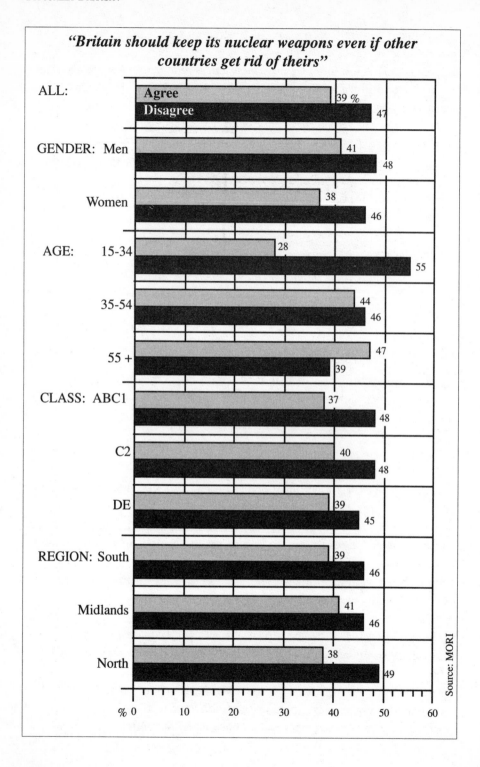

"Britain should keep its nuclear weapons even if other countries get rid of theirs"

ALL:
  Agree 39 %
  Disagree 47

GENDER: Men
  41
  48

Women
  38
  46

AGE: 15-34
  28
  55

35-54
  44
  46

55 +
  47
  39

CLASS: ABC1
  37
  48

C2
  40
  48

DE
  39
  45

REGION: South
  39
  46

Midlands
  41
  46

North
  38
  49

% 0   10   20   30   40   50   60

Source: MORI

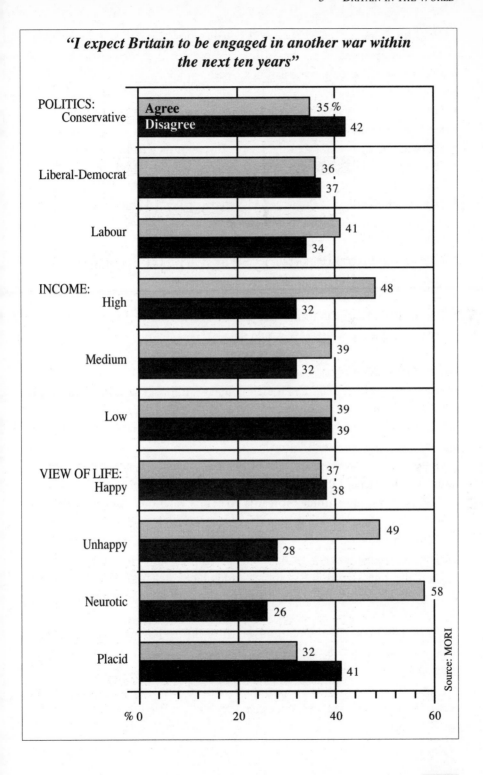

"I expect Britain to be engaged in another war within the next ten years"

POLITICS: Conservative — Agree 35%, Disagree 42
Liberal-Democrat — Agree 36, Disagree 37
Labour — Agree 41, Disagree 34
INCOME: High — Agree 48, Disagree 32
Medium — Agree 39, Disagree 32
Low — Agree 39, Disagree 39
VIEW OF LIFE: Happy — Agree 37, Disagree 38
Unhappy — Agree 49, Disagree 28
Neurotic — Agree 58, Disagree 26
Placid — Agree 32, Disagree 41

Source: MORI

Our fifth statement was: *"If I had the opportunity to emigrate I'd take it."*

The British have been travelling abroad to live for centuries. That wanderlust is still strong in the nation's blood.

- One person in ten strongly agreed with the statement (9%). A further 15% tended to agree.
- Overall, one person in four might leave Britain if they had the chance.
- Over half (62%) disagreed with the statement altogether and would not wish to leave home.
- More than one-third of the under-35s rated as potential emigrants.
- One in ten of the over-55s would join them.
- Politically, Labour supporters were most likely to want to leave Britain (28%), with Liberal Democrats second most likely (21%) and Conservatives least keen to go (18%).
- More Neurotics would emigrate than stay – 46% against 43%.
- But the Placids, true to form, were largely content where they were. Only 15% would leave while 71% would not.

Britain in Europe

Whatever the British think about their country's role and security in the world there is no doubt that, as 1992 looms and key decisions about the future political shape of the continent wait to be settled, they are increasingly sure that the nation belongs with Europe.

However, they are by no means of one mind about the past benefits or the future development of the Community.

We can compare attitudes towards Britain's relations with its allies and friends over an unusually long period, going as far back as 1969.

Then, and several times since, surveys have asked: *"Which of these – Europe, the Commonwealth or America – is the most important to Britain?"*

Over the intervening 22 years, attitudes have steadily evolved, towards Europe and away from the other two, especially the Commonwealth.

The trend is clear. The Commonwealth's rating has more than halved; America's has slipped by a third; and Europe's has risen more than one and a half times.

There have been blips. America recovered four points in importance between the last two surveys, once again probably reflecting its significance in the Gulf War.

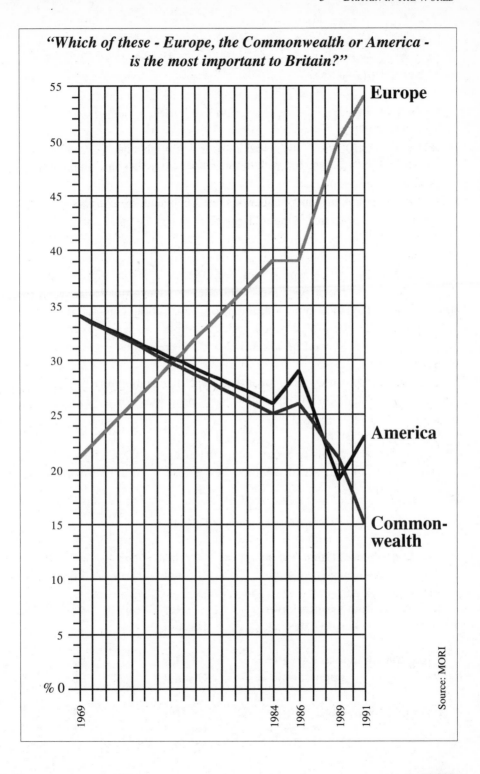

"Which of these - Europe, the Commonwealth or America - is the most important to Britain?"

Europe

America

Common-wealth

Source: MORI

- More men than women rated Europe most important – 62% to 48%.
- More of the middle age group took the same view – 63% of 35-54s; 55% of 15-34s and 46% of 55+s.
- The over-55s were still the most inclined to rate the Commonwealth high. One in five of them thought it most important to Britain against only one in ten of the 35-54s.
- Politically, more Conservatives than Labour supporters rated Europe most important – 58% to 53% – with Liberal Democrats at 59% marginally more enthusiastic than either.
- Labour supporters were not hankering after America or the Commonwealth. The gap between them and the Conservatives was made up of Labour Don't Knows.

The British may be becoming convinced that their destiny lies in Europe. But that does not mean they are experiencing an overwhelming rush of enthusiasm for the developing institutions of the European Community.

To explore the extent of Euro-enthusiasm we put two sets of propositions to our respondents, several of which we could make comparisons with from the past.

One set of propositions dealt with the impact the Community had already had on Britain and Europe; the other with proposals for developing the Community's institutions further.

First, the record so far.

We put four statements to people about the effects of the Community over the past few years and asked whether they agreed or disagreed with them. The statements were:

Britain's membership has:		%
Led to prices rising faster than they would have done	**Has**	**60**
	Has not	**20**
Reduced Britain's control over her own destiny	**Has**	**62**
	Has not	**24**
Given British industry greater opportunities	**Has**	**47**
	Has not	**38**
Increased the political stability of Europe	**Has**	**51**
	Has not	**26**

Source: MORI

- The highest levels of support were for the negative statements – that prices have risen fast and that Britain's control over her own destiny has been reduced.
- The most positive benefit people perceived was increased political stability. Support for this has grown steadily since 1977 when only 44% of people agreed with the same statement.
- Attitudes to two of the other statements have fluctuated around a fairly constant level of support. In 1977 63% thought membership had reduced Britain's control over its own destiny, against 1991's 62%, while in 1977 45% thought it had given British industry greater opportunities, against 1991's 47%.

Clearly, then, no signs of heady enthusiasm nor much indication that enthusiasm is on the increase.

But what about the future? Is there a greater eagerness for projects that have been talked about as possible building-blocks of the new Europe?

We put five such ideas to people and asked whether they supported or opposed them.

- More people liked the idea of European passports, integrated forces and a European Supreme Court than disliked them. But in no case did more than a modest majority support the proposal and fewer than half the total wanted a Supreme Court.
- The key issue of loss of sovereignty, with power being transferred to the European Parliament and away from individual national Parliaments, roused the biggest opposition. Fewer than one person in three wanted it and a majority were opposed.
- The other key issue, of a single European currency, roused less clearcut opposition. More than four people in ten were in favour. But still 2% more people were against the idea.
- Opinion on each of these issues has fluctuated over the four years back to 1987 with which we can make comparisons. But it has not shifted significantly. The biggest change was a 6% drop in support for a Supreme Court in the most recent 12-month period. (There is no comparable research on the question of a European currency.)

To sum up, we can say that people were broadly speaking more enthused about possible new developments in Europe, with the exception of more powers for a European Parliament and a single currency – than they were for

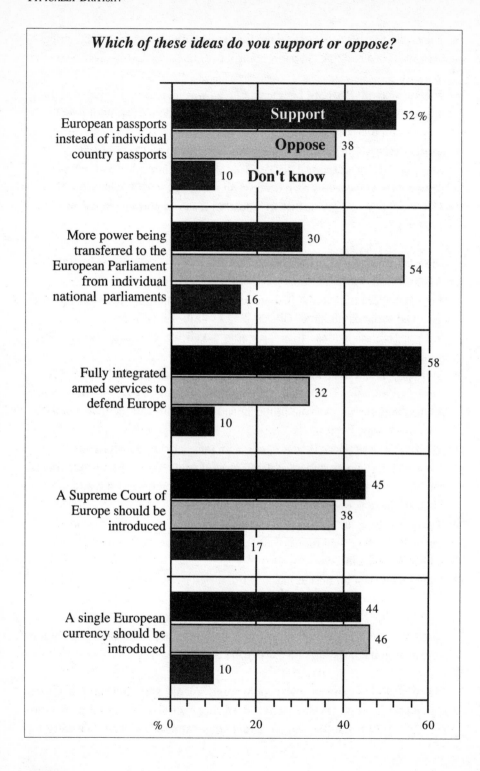

Which of these ideas do you support or oppose?

European passports instead of individual country passports
- **Support** 52 %
- **Oppose** 38
- **Don't know** 10

More power being transferred to the European Parliament from individual national parliaments
- 30
- 54
- 16

Fully integrated armed services to defend Europe
- 58
- 32
- 10

A Supreme Court of Europe should be introduced
- 45
- 38
- 17

A single European currency should be introduced
- 44
- 46
- 10

% 0 — 20 — 40 — 60

developments that have already taken place – again with one exception, greater political stability in Europe.

Who Are the Europeans?

Attitudes towards Europe are complex. For example, people who approved of what had already happened were by no means necessarily the same as those who looked forward to new developments.

- Women were consistently less keen on all European developments than men, whether it was a question of what had happened in the past or might in the future.

On one issue men and women were roughly matched: opposition to greater powers for a European Parliament. But the negative figure of – 24% net support by both sexes was reached only because twice as many women as men – 22% – had no opinion.

- Under-35s were generally more positive about Europe than older people, but not invariably.

Young people were less inclined than over-35s to believe that Britain's Community membership had caused prices to rise faster or reduced Britain's control over her own destiny. But the 35-54s gave greater support than older or younger people for the propositions that the Community had given greater political stability to Europe and brought British industry greater opportunities.

When it came to looking to the future, the youngest generation was keener than its elders on a European passport, more power for the European Parliament and a Supreme Court.

But the 35-54s were more supportive of a single European currency and the over-55s for fully integrated armed services.

- Political attitudes were also complex and apparently contradictory.

Labour supporters were generally more sceptical about past developments than Conservative. But they were also more enthusiastic about plans for the future. Liberal Democrats were enthusiasts for both past and future developments.

We can see this if we compare the net support of the parties with our two sets of questions (net support being the figure produced when we subtract opponents from supporters, ignoring those with no opinion).

Britain's membership of the Common Market has:		
Led to prices rising faster	*Conservative (net support)*	*36%*
	Labour	*51*
	Liberal Democrat	*28*
Reduced Britain's control over her own destiny	*Conservative*	*42*
	Labour	*40*
	Liberal Democrat	*29*
Given British industry greater opportunities	*Conservative*	*21*
	Labour	*1*
	Liberal Democrat	*17*
Increased the political stability of Europe	*Conservative*	*28*
	Labour	*26*
	Liberal Democrat	*35*

Source: MORI

On each count, except Europe's effect on Britain's destiny, Labour supporters showed themselves more sceptical than Conservatives or Liberal Democrats – in the case of rising prices and opportunites for British industry, dramatically so.

But when they looked to the future, attitudes were largely reversed. Now Labour supporters became less sceptical and Conservative more so.

This is how supporters of the major parties responded when we asked whether they would support or oppose ideas which, it was said, would bring Community member states closer together.

On each of these issues, Labour supporters showed more enthusiasm, or with the European Parliament less hostility, than supporters of the other parties. The widest gap was between Labour and Conservative supporters.

It is going to be a major problem for Britain's leaders to reconcile these cross-party differences between judgments of the past and future.

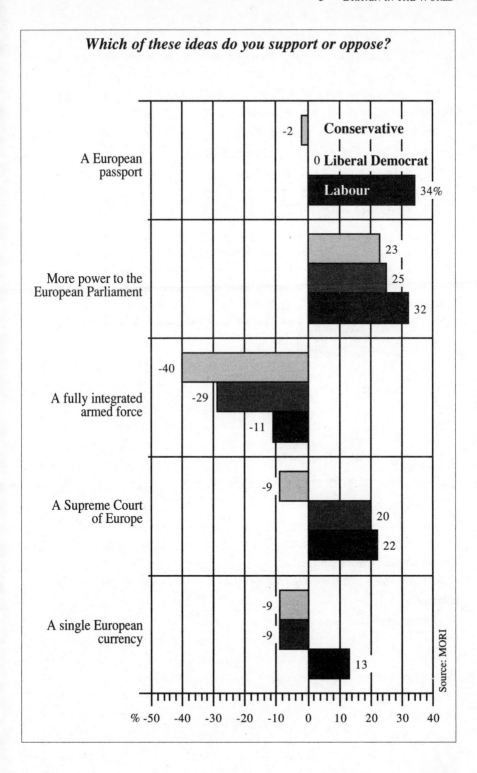

Which of these ideas do you support or oppose?

America in Retreat?

The British no longer regard America as having the same importance as 20 years ago.

But that does not mean they have started to dislike America or Americans. If anything, British liking for both has grown.

What is changing is people's perception of America as a model society, as a country the British themselves could learn from.

We put five statements about America to our respondents and we were able to compare their answers with others given five years earlier.

The first statement was: *"I like Americans as people."*

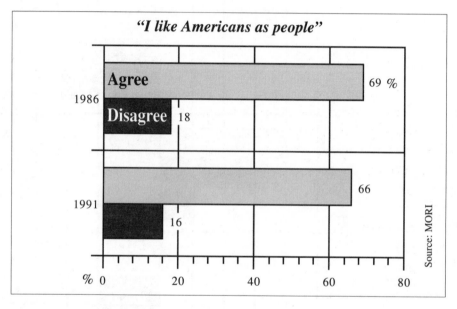

More women liked Americans (71%) than men (67%) and fewer women disliked them (15%) than men (21%).

But otherwise liking for Americans was consistent throughout the population.

The second statement was: *"I would like to go on holiday to America."*

1986	*Agree*	**64%**
	Disagree	**34**
1991	*Agree*	**69**
	Disagree	**29**

Source: MORI

Again the trend was up, but this time women were behind men in their enthusiasm. 3% more men than women would like to holiday in America and 4% more women than men would prefer not to.

The real enthusiasts for an America holiday were the young. Six in ten of the 15–34-year-olds (63%) would like to go there against four in ten of 35–54s (44%) and only one in ten of the over-55s (9%).

The third statement was: *"I think we can learn a great deal in this country from America."*

1986	*Agree*	**46%**	Source: MORI
	Disagree	**44**	
1991	*Agree*	**39**	
	Disagree	**54**	

Now we see the trend of opinion start to go down. 7% fewer people thought Britain could learn from America than had done five years before and a full 10% thought Britain could not learn from it.

The young were slightly more inclined than the older generations to think Britain had a great deal to learn from America but scepticism was fairly general.

The fourth statement was: *"I would like to live in America if I could not live in Britain."*

1986	*Agree*	**31%**	Source: MORI
	Disagree	**62**	
1991	*Agree*	**24**	
	Disagree	**72**	

The downward trend continues with another 7% fewer people agreeing with the statement and another 10% more people disagreeing.

Again, women were slightly more hostile than men (3% fewer would like to live in America) and the young were much the most enthusiastic. One in three people under 35 would like to live there if they were unable to stay at home, more than twice as many as the over-55s.

The fifth statement was: *"We would be better off if we were more like the Americans in many respects."*

1986	*Agree*	22%	
	Disagree	67	
1991	*Agree*	16	
	Disagree	78	

Source: MORI

Decline in support for this statement was exactly in line with the two previous ones and there were no major differences between groups.

The British, it seems, like America and Americans well enough. But they see no need to be like them.

Britons Abroad

Whatever the British think of the world, they can certainly claim to have seen a good deal of it.

More than eight adult Britons in ten have been abroad, mostly to Western Europe, but in large numbers to every corner of the globe.

When we asked which places people had visited, this is what they told us:

	%
A Western European country	66
America	19
An Eastern European country	17
Republic of Ireland	16
An African country	14
Middle East	13
Canada	10
Far East	9
India/Pakistan	7
Australia	6
South America	3
Soviet Union	2
None	16

Source: MORI

One person in ten had been to five or more of these destinations and one in 100 had been to ten or even all 12.

Women get the worst of it with travel. More men than women had been to every one of our destinations.

This is true even of such short and nowadays routine journeys as to Ireland (where 20% of men have been but only 13% of women) or Western Europe (72% men, 60% women).

But women need not necessarily envy men all their journeys. Many of the men's trips must have been on business. And a glance at the ages of people who have been to certain places suggests that much overseas travelling was not voluntary.

Twice as many over-55s had been to the Middle East as have under-35s (21% 55+, 6% 15–34) and three times as many to the Far East (13% against 4%) while twice as many had been to India and Pakistan (10% against 5%).

That seems odd. Have not travel opportunities greatly increased in the lifetimes of the under-35s?

Yes, but then we remember that when the oldest generation were young the British Empire was still alive. Many of their foreign trips must have been made years ago – in uniform as members of the forces.

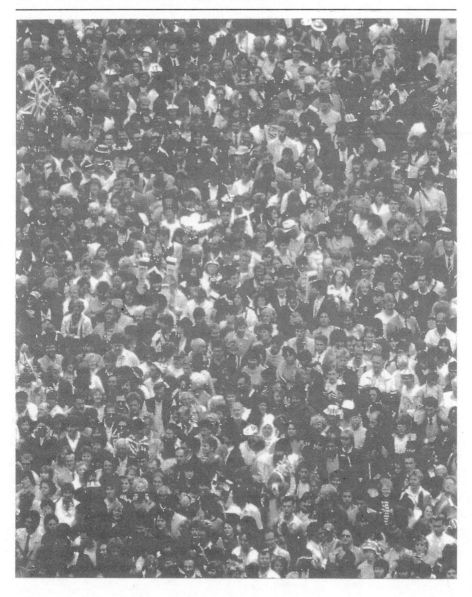

6 • PORTRAITS OF THE NATION

Being "typically British" is a hard idea to come to terms with.

How can any person be "typical" of such a richly diverse nation of individuals?

Yet people are well aware that, if they're typically anything, they are typically British and not French or American or Chinese.

It is the British Royal family they admire, the British Health Service they worry about, the British economy that makes them optimistic or pessimistic, the British class system they fit into somewhere.

But when people ask - how typical am I? - they do not mean how typical of all 44 million British adults. They are thinking of a smaller group of people. A group more or less like themselves.

What they want to know is how they rate and compare. Are they doing better or worse than other people like them? Are they richer or poorer, more fulfilled or less, participating in the same pleasures, even eating the same food?

Everybody wants to be their unique selves. But they also want to be like other people. Being an individual does not mean being so different from the rest that you become a total outsider.

To help you check how "typically British" you are in this sense, we have extracted from the huge mass of material in our survey a set of checklists so that at a glance you can tell how you compare with others. People like yourself and people not so like you.

If you are a young woman, for instance, you can discover how you compare with other young women. Or how different you are in your tastes and habits to young men. Or to older people of your own sex. Or to people who live in a different part of the country.

15 TO 34	WOMEN	MEN
MARITAL STATUS	%	%
Married	41	35
Living together	11	13
Single (including widowed/ divorced/separated)	48	52
CLASS		
ABC1	38	40
C2	34	32
DE	28	28
CHILDREN IN HOUSEHOLD		
Yes	62	37
No	38	63
WORK		
Full-time	31	72
Part-time	17	2
Not working	52	26
POLITICS		
Conservative	23	25
Labour	32	37
Liberal Democrat	16	13
INCOME		
High	12	14
Medium	29	37
Low	25	15
TRADE UNION MEMBER		
Yes	14	25
No	77	72
HOME OWNERSHIP		
Owned/mortgaged	56	65
Council tenant	28	25
Rent privately	10	7

15 TO 34	WOMEN	MEN
HAPPINESS	%	%
Very happy	33	30
Fairly happy	51	53
Neither happy nor unhappy	6	8
Fairly unhappy	6	6
Very unhappy	4	3

BEHAVIOUR

Most likely to have done in the past two days

Eaten fresh fruit	79	Eaten fresh fruit	69
Eaten fresh green vegetable	71	Eaten fresh green vegetable	67
Eaten wholemeal bread	58	Had an alcoholic drink	61
Eaten high-fibre/wholemeal cereal	46	Had sugar in tea/coffee	58
Drunk glass of whole milk	39	Eaten wholemeal bread	54
Had sugar in tea/coffee	39	Had fish & chips/fry-up	45
Had an alcoholic drink	36	Drunk glass of whole milk	45
Smoked	30	Taken part in sport	40

Most likely to have done in the past month

Watched TV/video	91	Watched TV/video	94
Gone shopping for food	86	Gone shopping for food	73
Read a book	62	Had takeaway meal/fast food	69
Had takeaway meal/fast food	60	Been to the pub	64
Been to the pub	55	General exercise/keep fit	57
General exercise/keep fit	52	Read book	50
Had friends round for meal/drink	49	Had friends round for meal/drink	49
Been for Sunday afternoon drive	45	DIY	48
Been to a restaurant	40	Been to a restaurant	45

Most likely to have been to in the past 12 months

Cinema	71	Cinema	68
Library	59	Library	53
Museum	34	Football match	43
Theatre	33	Pop concert	37
Pop concert	32	Museum	34
National Trust house/garden	31	National Trust house/garden	31
Art exhibition	22	Theatre	28
Pantomime	21	Modern dance	21

15 TO 34	WOMEN		MEN
	%		%

Most likely to have eaten in past month

Sunday roast	81	Sausages	82
Fish and chips	66	Fish and chips	81
Sausages	64	Pizza	80
Pizza	64	Bacon and eggs	80
Pasta	57	Sunday roast	79
Bacon and eggs	56	Pasta	69

SEX

How often do you have sexual intercourse

Four times a week or more	10	9
Two/three times a week	28	28
Once a week	10	16
Once a fortnight	3	2
Once a month	6	2
Never	21	21
Refused to answer	13	9
Don't know	9	13

How satisfying is sexual intercourse (% of all having intercourse)

Very satisfying	49	68
Fairly satisfying	47	30
Not very satisfying	3	0
Not at all satisying	0	1
Refused	1	1

How important do you think sexual love is in marriage

Very important	41	37
Fairly important	49	49
Not very important	6	4
Not at all important	0	1
Don't know	4	9

TOP CONCERNS

Education/schools	46	Unemployment	49
Unemployment/factory closures	45	NHS	39
Crime/law and order	43	Crime	37
NHS/hospitals	40	Education/schools	37
Pollution/environment	40	Pollution/environment	34
AIDS	39	AIDS	33

35 TO 44	WOMEN	MEN
MARITAL STATUS	%	%
Married	81	74
Living together	4	10
Single (including widowed/ divorced/separated)	15	16
CLASS		
ABC1	55	47
C2	29	28
DE	16	25
CHILDREN IN HOUSEHOLD		
Yes	60	59
No	40	41
WORK		
Full-time	39	86
Part-time	27	1
Not working	34	13
POLITICS		
Conservative	44	29
Labour	27	40
Liberal Democrat	13	13
INCOME		
High	23	30
Medium	40	42
Low	15	12
TRADE UNION MEMBER		
Yes	18	43
No	76	54
HOME OWNERSHIP		
Owned/mortgaged	81	77
Council tenant	16	17
Rent privately	3	2

35 TO 44	WOMEN	MEN
HAPPINESS	%	%
Very happy	31	18
Fairly happy	53	55
Neither happy nor unhappy	9	16
Fairly unhappy	4	10
Very unhappy	3	1

BEHAVIOUR

Most likely to have done in the past two days

Women		Men	
Eaten fresh green vegetables	90	Eaten fresh green vegetables	76
Eaten fresh fruit	87	Eaten fresh fruit	71
Eaten wholemeal bread	62	Had alcoholic drink	66
Eaten high-fibre/wholemeal cereal	52	Eaten wholemeal bread	50
Had alcoholic drink	48	Sugar in tea/coffee	49
Had sugar in tea/coffee	41	Smoked cigarette etc	43
Smoked cigarette, etc	38	Drunk glass whole milk	38
Taken painkiller (eg aspirin)	38	Eaten high-fibre cereal = fish and chips	37

Most likely to have done in the past month

Women		Men	
Gone shopping for food	97	Watched TV/video	88
Watched TV/video	94	Gone shopping for food	86
Read a book	72	Gardening	77
Had friends for meal/drink	67	Been to pub	70
Gardening	64	Had takeaway meal/fast food	66
Been to a restaraunt	57	DIY	63
Had takeaway meal/fast food	57	Read a book	61
Read nutritional information	50	Been to a restaurant	58
General exercise/keep fit	47	Been for Sunday drive	41

Most likely to have been to in the past 12 months

Women		Men	
Library	70	Museum	62
Cinema	56	Library	56
Theatre	55	Cinema	49
Museum	54	Theatre	45
National Trust house/garden	50	National Trust house/garden	44
Art exhibition	31	Art exhibition	29
Pantomime	25	Football match	24
Pop concert	20	Pop concert	17

35 TO 44	WOMEN		MEN
	%		%

Most likely to have eaten in past month

Sunday roast	90	Fish and chips	87
Pasta	74	Sunday roast	86
Fish and chips	70	Sausages	83
Pizza	66	Bacon and eggs	77
Bacon and eggs	65	Chinese meal	67
Sausages	64	Pizza	64

SEX
How often have sexual intercourse

Four times a week or more	4	10
Two/three times a week	29	31
Once a week	20	21
Once a fortnight	7	3
Once a month	7	4
Never	7	5
Refused to answer	14	19
Don't know	12	7

How satisfying is sexual intercourse (per cent of all having intercourse)

Very satisfying	45	37
Fairly satisfying	51	60
Not very satisfying	3	2
Not at all satisfying	2	0
Refused to answer	0	0
Don't know	0	1

How important do you think sexual love is in marriage

Very important	36	45
Fairly important	48	47
Not very important	8	5
Not at all important	2	0
Don't know	6	3

TOP CONCERNS

NHS/hospitals	52	Crime/law and order	54
Education/schools	51	Unemployment	47
Crime/law and order	47	NHS/hospitals	47
Unemployment/factory closures	46	Education/schools	42
Pollution/environment	42	Pollution/environment	37
Drug Abuse	31	Inflation/prices	34

45 TO 64	WOMEN		MEN
MARITAL STATUS	%		%
Married	72		82
Living together	3		2
Single (including widowed/ divorced/separated)	25		16
CLASS			
ABC1	45		41
C2	26		28
DE	29		31
CHILDREN IN HOUSEHOLD			
Yes	6		12
No	94		88
WORK			
Full-time	27		64
Part-time	21		2
Not working	52		34
POLITICS			
Conservative	37		30
Labour	32		36
Liberal Democrat	14		15
INCOME			
High	9		14
Medium	27		36
Low	37		26
TRADE UNION MEMBER			
Yes	14		39
No	80		58
HOME OWNERSHIP			
Owned/mortgaged	71		81
Council tenant	21		17
Rent privately	5		2

45 TO 64	WOMEN	MEN

HAPPINESS

	%	%
Very happy	27	31
Fairly happy	47	44
Neither happy nor unhappy	13	10
Fairly unhappy	11	10
Very unhappy	2	5

BEHAVIOUR

Most likely to have done in the past two days

Eaten fresh fruit	87	Eaten fresh green vegetables	83
Eaten fresh green vegetables	79	Eaten fresh fruit	73
Eaten wholemeal bread	68	Eaten wholemeal bread	61
Eaten high-fibre cereal	58	Had sugar in tea/coffee	56
Taken painkiller (eg aspirin)	44	Had an alcoholic drink	56
Taken any medicine	41	Eaten high-fibre cereal	51
Had an alcoholic drink	39	Taken any medicine	38
Had sugar in tea/coffee	37	Had fish and chips/fry-up	36

Most likely to have done in the past month

Gone shopping for food	92	Watched TV/video	91
Watched TV/video	87	Gone shopping for food	80
Read a book	70	Gardening	71
Gardening	66	DIY	67
Had friends round	54	Read a book	62
Been to a restaurant	47	Been to the pub	49
Been out for Sunday drive	40	Been to restaurant	43
Read nutritional information	37	Had friends round	40
Been to pub	31	Been out for Sunday drive	34

Most likely to have done in the past 12 months

National Trust house/garden	49	Library	47
Library	48	National Trust house/garden	43
Theatre	46	Museum	41
Museum	39	Theatre	38
Art exhibition	27	Cinema	30
Cinema	27	Art exhibition	23
Modern dance	16	Football match	21
Pantomime	16	Orchestral concert	17

45 to 64	WOMEN		MEN
	%		%

Most likely to have eaten in past month

Sunday roast	84	Sunday roast	90
Bacon and eggs	72	Fish and chips	85
Fish and chips	69	Bacon and eggs	83
Sausages	66	Sausages	77
Pasta	43	Pizza	47
Chinese meal = Porridge	40	Chinese meal	44

SEX

How often have sexual intercourse

Four times a week or more	0	1
Two/three times a week	9	17
Once a week	13	20
Once a fortnight	7	9
Once a month	8	10
Never	31	13
Refused to answer	22	20
Don't know	10	10

How satisfying is sexual intercourse (percent of all having intercourse)

Very satisfying	44	57
Fairly satisfying	47	38
Not very satisfying	2	1
Not at all satisfying	5	1
Refused to answer	2	1
Don't know	0	2

How important do you think sexual love is in marriage

Very important	35	38
Fairly important	48	50
Not very important	9	3
Not at all important	2	0
Don't know	6	9

TOP CONCERNS

NHS/hospitals	58	Crime/law and order	52
Crime/law and order	57	Unemployment	46
Unemployment	35	NHS/hospitals	43
Pollution/environment	33	Inflation/prices	35
Inflation/prices	28	Pollution/environment	35
Drug abuse	27	Education/schools	30

65+	WOMEN	MEN
MARITAL STATUS	%	%
Married	33	69
Living together	0	0
Single (including widowed/ divorced/separated)	67	31
CLASS		
ABC1	27	41
C2	19	20
DE	54	39
CHILDREN IN HOUSEHOLD		
Yes	1	3
No	99	97
WORK		
Full-time	0	3
Part-time	0	3
Not working	100	94
POLITICS		
Conservative	39	32
Labour	29	38
Liberal Democrat	13	15
INCOME		
High	4	5
Medium	2	12
Low	63	56
TRADE UNION MEMBER		
Yes	2	5
No	85	84
HOME OWNERSHIP		
Owned/mortgaged	58	60
Council tenant	36	36
Rent privately	3	2

65+	WOMEN		MEN
HAPPINESS	%		%
Very happy	24		35
Fairly happy	52		49
Neither happy nor unhappy	12		8
Fairly unhappy	7		7
Very unhappy	5		1

BEHAVIOUR

Most likely to have done in the past two days

Eaten fresh fruit	86	Eaten fresh green vegetables	82
Eaten fresh green vegetables	82	Eaten fresh fruit	79
Eaten wholemeal bread	63	Eaten wholemeal bread	60
Eaten high-fibre cereal	49	Taken any medicine	56
Taken any medicine	47	Had sugar in tea/coffee	55
Taken painkiller (eg aspirin)	39	Eaten high-fibre cereal	53
Had sugar in tea/coffee	31	Had an alcoholic drink	52
Had an alcoholic drink	26	Had fish and chips/fry-up	38

Most likely to have done in the past month

Gone shopping for food	88	Watched TV/video	83
Watched TV/video	86	Gone shopping for food	80
Read a book	68	Gardening	75
Gardening	54	Read a book	69
Had friends round for meal/drink	44	Had friends round	43
Been to a restaurant	37	DIY	42
Been for Sunday drive	29	Been to a restaurant	37
Read nutritional information	26	Been to the pub	31
Been away for weekend	13	Been for Sunday drive	28

Most likely to have been to in the past 12 months

Library	47	Library	53
National Trust house/garden	32	National Trust house/garden	41
Theatre	25	Museum	39
Museum	18	Theatre	26
Art exhibition	17	Art exhibition	23
Pantomime	14	Orchestral concert	15
Orchestral concert	12	Cinema	15
Opera/Cinema	10	Football match	15

65+	WOMEN		MEN
	%		%

Most likely to have eaten in past month

Sunday roast	85	Sunday roast	82
Bacon and eggs	69	Bacon and eggs	77
Fish and chips	67	Sausages	76
Sausages	64	Fish and chips	70
Porridge	46	Porridge	48
Pasta	23	Pizza	25

SEX

How often have sexual intercourse

Four times a week or more	0	1
Two/three times a week	1	2
Once a week	2	2
Once a fortnight	1	3
Once a month	5	9
Never	65	49
Refused to answer	13	18
Don't know	13	14

How satisfying is sexual intercourse (per cent of all having intercourse)

Very satisfying	36	47
Fairly satisfying	44	48
Not very satisfying	10	0
Not at all satisfying	10	0
Refused to answer	0	0
Don't know	0	5

How important think sexual love is in marriage

Very important	30	39
Fairly important	44	40
Not very important	7	8
Not at all important	5	3
Don't know	14	10

TOP CONCERNS

NHS/hospitals	48	NHS/hospitals	52
Crime/law and order	45	Crime/law and order	50
Pensions/social security	42	Pensions/social security	43
Inflation/prices	33	Inflation/prices	39
Unemployment	29	Pollution/environment	29
Pollution/environment	26	Drug abuse	28
=Drug abuse			

REGIONAL PROFILES	NORTH	MIDLANDS	SOUTH
	%	%	%
MARITAL STATUS			
Married	57	55	58
Living together	4	6	8
Single/separated/divorced	39	39	34
CLASS			
ABC1	34	36	49
C2	28	31	27
DE	38	33	24
CHILDREN IN HOUSEHOLD			
Yes	30	31	30
No	70	69	70
WORK			
Full time	40	45	42
Part time	9	7	11
Not working	51	48	47
VOTING INTENTION			
Conservative	27	28	37
Labour	42	35	26
Liberal Democrat	10	16	17
INCOME			
Low	9	12	17
Medium	25	27	33
High	31	33	27
TRADE UNION MEMBER			
Yes	25	18	17
No	67	74	78
HOME OWNERSHIP			
Owned/mortgage	66	72	66
Council tenant	27	23	23
Rent privately	5	3	7
HAPPINESS			
Very happy	28	31	29
Fairly happy	50	50	50
Neither happy nor unhappy	9	12	10
Fairly unhappy	10	4	8
Very unhappy	3	3	3

NORTH		MIDLANDS		SOUTH	
BEHAVIOUR	%		%		%

Most likely to have done in the past two days

NORTH		MIDLANDS		SOUTH	
Fresh fruit	78	Green vegetables	79	Fresh fruit	79
Green vegetables	76	Fresh fruit	77	Green vegetables	77
Wholemeal bread	60	Wholemeal bread	60	Wholemeal bread	60
Alcoholic drink	49	High fibre cereal	47	High fibre cereal	51
Sugar in tea/coffee	46	Alcoholic drink	47	Sugar in tea/coffee	47
High-fibre cereal	45	Sugar in tea/coffee	44	Alcoholic drink	46
Fish & chips	35	Fish & chips	34	Taken medicine	33
Smoked cigarette/pipe or Taken painkiller	32	Drunk whole milk	33	Taken pain killer	32

Most likely to have done in the past month

NORTH		MIDLANDS		SOUTH	
Watched TV/video	91	TV/video	88	TV/video	89
Been food shopping	85	Been food shopping	83	Been food shopping	84
Read a book	60	Gardening	63	Read a book	68
Been to the pub	51	Read a book	59	Gardening	59
Gardening	49	Been to the pub	49	Friends round	52
Friends round	47	Friends round	45	Takeaway	47
Restaurant	44	Restaurant	43	Restaurant	46
Takeaway	40	Takeaway	41	DIY	41
Sunday afternoon drive	36	DIY	41	Pub	40

Most likely to have been to in the past twelve months

NORTH		MIDLANDS		SOUTH	
Library	49	Library	51	Library	58
Cinema	44	Cinema	42	Cinema	45
Museum	38	NT House/Garden	39	NT House/Garden	43
NT House/Garden	34	Theatre	33	Museum	42
Theatre	32	Museum	32	Theatre	40
Football match	21	Art exhibition	20	Art exhibition	28
Art exhibition	19	Football match	19	Pop concert	19
Pantomime	18	Modern dance	17	Football match	17

Most likely to have eaten in the past month

NORTH		MIDLANDS		SOUTH	
Sunday roast	80	Sunday roast	89	Sunday roast	84
Fish & chips	77	Fish & chips	78	Sausages	72
Bacon & eggs	75	Sausages	74	Bacon & eggs	71
Sausages	70	Bacon & eggs	70	Fish & chips	69
Pizza	49	Pizza	49	Pasta	58
Pasta	45	Chinese meal	46	Pizza	55

REGIONAL PROFILES	NORTH	MIDLANDS	SOUTH
SEX			
How often have sexual intercourse			
Four times a week or more	4	6	5
Two/three times a week	19	15	22
Once a week	15	10	13
Once a fortnight	4	2	6
Once a month	6	5	6
Never	26	24	28
Refused to answer	15	19	13
Don't know	11	19	7
How satisfying is sexual intercourse (% of all having intercourse)			
Very satisfying	53	58	47
Fairly satisfying	43	38	46
Not very important	1	1	3
Not at all satisfying	2	1	1
Refused to answer	0	0	1
Don't know	1	2	2
How important do you think sexual love is in marriage			
Very important	39	31	40
Fairly important	49	43	49
Not very important	6	6	6
Not at all important	2	1	1
Don't know	4	9	4

TOP CONCERNS	NORTH		MIDLANDS		SOUTH
Crime	50	NHS	47	NHS	46
NHS	46	Crime	46	Crime	45
Unemployment	41	Unemployment	43	Unemployment	41
Environment	31	Environment	33	Pollution	39
Drug abuse	28	Education	31	Education	39
Education/Inflation	28	Drug abuse	30	Inflation	30

7 • BRITISH ACTIVISTS

We have identified a series of British types which we have labelled according to the characteristics they showed in response to certain of our questions. If you think you are a Green enthusiast, a pro-European, a Neurotic or any of our other types, see how your profile matches up with others like you in the table that follows.

We have defined as:

Neurotics, those who worried a great deal about five or more statements at Question 7 in our survey.

Placids, those who were not worried a great deal about any of those statements.

Green Activists said they had done five or more of the activities at Question 36, excluding the use of unleaded petrol and owning a pet.

Leisurists had done ten or more activities at Question 40, excluding activities m, n, o, u, v, w, x and y.

Socialisers had done five or more from items c, g, h, i, k, l, r, t at Question 40.

Culturalists had attended five or more events at Question 35, excluding m.

Healthists had consumed five or more of items a, b, c, d, f, j, k at Question 39.

Socio-Political Activists had done five or more of the activities at Question 44.

Pro-Europeans agreed with all five statements at Question 32.

BRITISH PUBLIC 100%	ALL	GREEN ACTIVISTS 25% = 100%	LEISURISTS 12% = 100%	SOCIALISERS 9% = 100%	CULTURALISTS 21% = 100%	HEALTHISTS 20% = 100%	SOCIO-POLITICAL ACTIVISTS 8% = 100%	NEUROTICS 8% = 100%	PLACIDS 40% = 100%	PRO-EUROPEAN 13% = 100%
48	Men	39	62	51	50	50	56	42	50	56
52	Women	61	38	49	50	50	44	58	50	44
37	15-34	41	52	63	44	50	21	57	35	39
29	35-54	37	34	28	36	26	42	22	27	31
33	55+	22	14	9	20	24	36	21	38	30
41	ABC1	60	59	59	68	50	62	31	43	43
28	C2	24	27	26	16	24	19	28	28	24
31	DE	16	14	14	16	26	19	41	28	33
35	North	27	29	42	32	30	29	31	36	31
25	Midlands	27	28	25	20	27	28	27	25	27
40	South	46	43	33	48	43	43	42	39	42
22	Own home	18	19	21	23	19	31	15	26	24
45	Mortgage	55	59	55	57	54	51	34	46	46
25	Council tenant	16	10	10	10	17	16	42	20	20
5	Rent privately	6	9	10	6	7	0	7	5	7
20	Trade unionist	20	24	24	22	17	25	13	20	24
42	Work full time	45	58	63	47	46	47	36	43	45
9	Work part time	12	9	5	10	8	9	10	9	8
49	Not working	43	33	32	43	46	44	55	47	47
18	Work (public sector)	19	27	26	19	19	28	14	18	16
33	Work (private sector)	37	40	42	38	33	28	30	34	36
31	Conservative	32	36	27	36	31	27	11	36	22
34	Labour	28	29	36	28	30	35	48	28	46
14	Liberal Democrat	21	15	15	15	16	23	10	16	16

8 • Social Class Definitions

A   Professionals such as doctors, surgeons, solicitors or dentists; chartered people like architects; fully qualified people with a large degree of responsibility such as senior editors, senior civil servants, town clerks, senior business executives and managers, and high-ranking grades of the Services.

B   People with very responsible jobs such as university lecturers, matrons of hospitals, heads of local government departments; middle management in business; qualified scientists, bank managers and upper grades of the Services, police inspectors.

C1 All others doing non-manual jobs; nurses, technicians, pharmacists, salesmen, publicans, people in clerical positions and middle ranks of the Services, police sergeants.

C2 Skilled manual workers/craftsmen who have served apprenticeships; foremen, manual workers with special qualifications such as long-distance lorry drivers, security officers and lower grades of Services/police constables.

D   Semi-skilled and unskilled manual workers, including labourers and mates of occupations in the C2 grade and people serving apprenticeships; machine minders, farm labourers, bus and railway conductors, laboratory assistants, postmen, waiter/waitress, door-to-door and van salesmen.

E   Those on lowest levels of subsistence including pensioners, casual workers, and others with minimum levels of income.

9 • QUESTIONNAIRE

MORI/6449   Serial No ....
(1–4)   OUO   (5–8)
CARD 1 _____ 9

Living in Britain

Fieldwork carried out between 11 April and
2 May 1991

Total number of interviews: 1230

Marked–up questionnaire with weighted
data

Telephone: Yes (Write in No) 1 (10)

....

No 2   10

Constituency Name ....

Constituency Number:

(11) (12) (13) (14) (15) (16)   11–16

Sex of Respondent   %
Male 48
Female 52

Age of Respondent   %
15–17 5
18–24 13
25–34 20
35–39 9
40–44 10
45–54 12
55–59 5
60–64 7
65–74 12
75+ 7

Respondent is   %
Head of household 53
Not head of household 47

Working Status of HOH   %
Full–time (30+hrs/wk+) 61
Part–time (8–29 hrs) 2
Not working (ie under 8hrs/wk)
– housewife 6
– retired 22
– unemployed (registered) 4
– unemployed (not registered)
   but looking for work) 1
– student 2
– other 1

IF HOH WORKING: HOH works in
%
Public sector 18
Private sector 44

Head of Household if working is %
Self–employed 11
Not self–employed 49

Occupation of Head of Household
Position/Rank/Grade

....

Industry/Type of Firm

....

Quals/Degree/Apprenticeships

....

Number of staff Responsible for

....

REMEMBER TO PROBE CWE/PENSION

Class (CODE FROM HOH OCCUPN ABOVE)
%
A 2
B 16
C1 25
C2 28
D 18
E 11

Working status of respondent   %
Full–time (30+hrs/wk+) 35
Part–time (8–29 hrs) 10
Not working (ie under 8hrs/wk)
– housewife 16
– retired 15
– unemployed (registered) 4
– unemployed (not registered)
   but looking for work) 1
– student 5
– other 1

RESPONDENT IF WORKING: works in
%
Public sector 15
Private Sector 25

Respondent if working is: %
Self–employed 5
Not self–employed 34

Respondent's own Occupation (If not HOH)
Position/Rank/Grade

....

Industry/Type of Firm

....

Quals/Degree/Apprenticeships

....

Number of staff Responsible for

....

Class (CODE FROM OWN OCCUPN ABOVE)
%
A .... *
B 3
C1 11
C2 5
D 10
E .... *

Respondent is
	%
Trade union member	20
Not trade union member	73
No answer	5

No in household (incl respondent)

Adults (aged 15+)   1 2 3 4 5 6 7 8 9+

Children (under 15) 0 1 2 3 4 5 6 7 8 9+

Ages of Children (in household)
	%
Aged 0–4	17
Aged 5–8	13
Aged 9–10	7
Aged 11–14	11
No children under 15	67

Home is
	%
Being bought on mortgage	46
Owned outright by household	22
Rented from Local Authority	24
Rented from private landlord	5
Other (WRITE IN & CODE '5')	1

....

Household Income SHOWCARD R (R)
Could you please give me the letter from this card for the group in which you would place your total household income from all sources, before tax and other deductions.
	%
A	2
B	8
C	6
D	4
E	4
F	5
G	7
H	5
I	6
J	12
K	13
Refused	21

Daily Newspaper readership
SHOWCARD S (R)
	%
Daily Express	8
Daily Mail	12
Daily Mirror/Record	20
Glasgow Herald	2
Daily Telegraph	6
Financial Times	1
The Guardian	4
The Independent	4
The Scotsman	1
The Star	4
The Sun	22
The Times	2
The Evening Standard	2
Today	3
None of these	31

Sunday Newspaper readership
SHOWCARD T (R)
	%
Independent on Sunday	4
News of the World	23
Sunday Express	9
Sunday Mail (Scotland only)	7
Sunday Mirror	12
Sunday Post	7
Sunday Sport	1
Sunday Telegraph	3
The Mail on Sunday	13
The Observer	3
The Sunday People	11
The Sunday Times	6
Scotland on Sunday	1
None of these	29

Car Driving (Respondent)
	%
Every/most days	55
Sometimes (less than 1/fortnight)	7
Never	37

How often do you watch television these days? Would it be nearer to 5 or more days, (PROBE: Do you view 5, 6 or 7 days) 3 or 4 days a week, 1 or 2 days a week or less often?
	%
Never	1
Less than 1 day a week	*
1 day a week	1
2 days a week	3
3 days a week	3
4 days a week	2
5 days a week	4
6 days a week	1
7 days a week	85

On a day when you do watch, for how many hours do you watch television?
	%
1 hour or less	6
Over 1, up to 2 hours	22
Over 2, up to 3 hours	28
Over 3, up to 4 hours	18
Over 4, up to 5 hours	12
Over 5, up to 6 hours	8
Over 6, up to 7 hours	4
Over 7, up to 8 hours	*
Over 8, up to 9 hours	1
Over 9 hours a day	2

TV Area Normally Watched
SHOWCARD U (R)
	%
North East (TyneTeess)	6
Lancashire (Granada)	12
Yorkshire	11
Midlands (Central)	17
Wales and West (Harlech HTV)	7
East Anglia (Anglia)	9
London	19
Southern (TVS)	6
South West (TSW)	2
Border TV	0
Grampian TV	1
Scottish TV	9
Don't know	*

– 3 –

Respondent willing to be re-interviewed

	%
Yes	78
No	21

Interviewer Declaration

I confirm that I have conducted this interview face-to-face with the above named person and that I have asked all relevant questions fully, recorded the answers and checked the coding, confirming to the survey specification, within the MRS code of Conduct.

Interviewer Name:

....

Interviewer Number ☐ ☐ ☐ ☐ ☐
(44) (45) (46) (47) (48)
44–48

Date of interview (WRITE IN) ....

Length of interview (mins) ☐ ☐
(49) (50)
49–50

INTERVIEW STARTS HERE
ALL DEMOGRAPHIC QUESTIONS (EXCEPT THOSE NECESSARY TO CHECK THAT THE RESPONDENT FITS YOUR QUOTA), MUST BE ASKED AT THE END OF THE INTERVIEW. NAME, ADDRESS AND TELEPHONE NUMBER MAY BE ASKED AT THE BEGINNING OR THE END

"INTERVIEWER: SOME SHOWCARDS HAVE BEEN REVERSED. SHOWCARDS WHICH MAY BE REVERSED ARE MARKED (R) ON THE QUESTIONNAIRE. PLEASE BE CAREFUL TO CODE THE CORRECT RESPONSE"

Good Morning/Afternoon/Evening. My name is . . . and I am conducting a MORI poll about what kinds of things people do and think about in Britain nowadays. Firstly could I ask you . . .

Q1 How would you vote if there was a General Election tomorrow?
(IF AGE 15–17 ADD: If you were old enough to vote?) CODE BELOW

IF UNDECIDED OR REFUSED AT Q1
Q2 Which party are you most inclined to support?

Base:	Q1 (1230)		Q2 (255)	
	%		%	
Conservative	27		20	
Labour	29	GO	21	
Lib Dem	12	TO	13	GO
Scot/Welsh Nat	1	Q3	2	
Green Party	1		3	TO
Other	*		–	
Would not vote	9		1	Q3
Undecided	18	GO TO	28	
Refused	2	Q2	14	

Q3 Do you think that the general economic condition of the country will improve, stay the same, or get worse over the next 12 months?

	%
Improve	36
Stay the same	26
Get worse	33
Don't know	5

173

Q4   **Overall, how happy or unhapppy are you with your life at present?**

	%
Very happy	29
Fairly happy	50
Neither happy nor unhappy	10
Fairly unhappy	7
Very unhappy	3
No opinion	*

Q5   **Would you say you are likely to be financially better off, worse off or about the same in the year 2000 as you are now?**

	%	
Better off	45	ASK Q5a
Worse off	17	GO TO Q5b
About the same	28	GO TO
Don't know	10	Q6

IF BETTER OFF ASK Q5a

Q5a   **What are the main reasons you believe you will be better off?**

Base: All who think they will be financially better off in the year 2000 (576)

	%	
New job/change of job	33	
Savings/investment	10	
Promotion	13	
General increase in pay	25	GO
Inheritance	2	
Marriage	2	TO
Luck/win pools	*	
Children leave home/fewer dependents	9	Q6
Will have paid off mortgage	7	
Increased value of home	4	
Other (WRITE IN AND CODE X)	33	

....

No opinion	1

IF WORSE OFF ASK Q5b

Q5b   **What are the main reasons you believe you will be worse off?**

Base: All who think they will be financially worse off in the year 2000 (199)

	%
Loss of job	9
Marriage	1
Retirement	23
Divorce	–
Death	1
Fixed income/income rise less than inflation	31
Spending more than income/using up savings	11
Reduced income generally	14
Starting/raising family	2
Taking out mortgage	1
Higher expenses generally	22
Other (WRITE IN AND CODE Y)	24

....

No opinion	2

Q6 SHOWCARD A (R) **Here is a list of things some people have told us concern them. Which would you say are the four or five that concern you most? Just read out the letters.**

		%
a)	AIDS	24
b)	Britain's relationship with America	3
c)	Common Market/EEC	7
d)	Crime/law & order/violence/vandalism	47
e)	Defence/foreign affairs	2
f)	Drug abuse	27
g)	Economy/economic situation	13
h)	Education/schools	33
i)	Housing	14
j)	Inflation/prices	29
k)	Local government/rate capping/poll tax	19
l)	Morality/permissiveness	8
m)	National Health Service/hospitals	46
n)	Northern Ireland	9
o)	Nuclear power/fuels	9
p)	Nuclear weapons/nuclear war/disarmament	13
q)	Pensions/social security	19
r)	Pollution/Environment	35
s)	Pound/exchange–rate/value of pound	4
t)	Privatisation	6
u)	Race relations/immigration/immigrants	11
v)	Taxation	13
w)	Trade union/strikes	3
x)	Unemployment/factory closures/lack of industry	41

Other (WRITE IN & CODE '1') 1

....

None of these 1
Don't know .... *

Q7 SHOWCARD B (R) **I am going to read out things that some people worry about these days, and I would like you to tell me from this card to what extent, if at all, you have worried about each one in the last 2–3 weeks. READ OUT. ROTATE ORDER. TICK START (√)**

		A great deal %	A fair amount %	A little %	Not at all %	Does not apply %	No opinion %
a)	Not having enough money	20	19	28	32	*	1
b)	The education of children	17	21	19	22	20	1
c)	Unemployment of yourself or members of your family	20	16	19	39	6	*
d)	Nuclear war/world war	13	14	21	51	*	1
e)	Your health/your family's health	18	23	29	29	*	*
f)	Relations with your neighbours	2	6	13	78	1	*
g)	Your children	15	13	15	28	28	1
h)	Relations with your husband/wife/ boy/girlfriend	8	7	11	53	20	1
i)	How things are going at work	7	12	15	21	43	1
j)	Growing old	4	8	23	63	1	*
k)	Vandalism/crime in this area	19	23	31	27	*	*
l)	Your housing conditions	7	10	15	66	1	1

CARD 2   9

Q8   SHOWCARD C (R)   Which two or three items on this list do you think are the <u>most important</u> for you personally in determining how happy or unhappy you are in general these days? Just read out the letters. CODE BELOW

Q9   SHOWCARD D (R)   I am going to read out a list of things which can affect how happy people are. From this card I would like you to tell me how happy or unhappy you are with each one? READ DOWN LIST (a–k)

	Q8 Impor-tant %	Extrem-ely happy %	Very happy %	Fairly happy %	Q9 Neither happy nor unhappy %	Fairly unhappy %	Very unhappy %	Extrem-ely unhappy %
a) District you live in	15	7	37	41	7	4	1	1
b) Education you received	7	4	24	43	11	9	4	1
c) Your family life	41	15	50	26	5	1	1	
d) Health	59	7	33	40	7	7	2	1
e) Housing conditions	9	9	44	31	5	5	2	1
f) Job/employment of you/ your family	31	4	26	34	16	9	5	2
g) Marriage/partner	35	19	35	15	18	2	1	1
h) How you use your spare time	14	6	29	42	11	6	2	*
i) Standard of living	30	4	30	46	7	7	2	1
j) Your weight	13	4	20	33	13	16	7	3
k) Financial investments/money	25	1	10	41	22	13	5	2

Q10   Are you:

	%
Married	57
Living with someone as if you were married	6
Divorced	4
Widowed	11
Separated	2
Single, but engaged	2
Single, not engaged	18

Q11   Have you ever lived with someone as if you were married (IF APPLICABLE: other than the person you are living with at the moment)?

	%
Yes	16
No	81
Refused	3

Q12   If you had a choice, would you rather be a man or a woman?

	%
A man	53
A woman	42
Don't know	5

- 7 -

Q13 SHOWCARD E (R) Which 3 or 4 things on this list do you think men in general like most in a woman? Just read out the letters next to the appropriate phrases. CODE BELOW

Q14 SHOWCARD E (R) AGAIN Which 3 or 4 things do you think women in general like most in a man? Again, just read out the letters. CODE BELOW

		Q13 %	Q14 %
a)	Intelligence	36	38
b)	Femininity/masculinity	28	18
c)	Self–confidence	21	30
d)	Modesty	8	6
e)	A sense of humour	64	60
f)	Sexiness	32	8
g)	Common sense	39	33
h)	Good looks	50	33
i)	A sense of style	15	14
j)	Cuddliness	10	5
k)	A sense of independence	17	14
l)	Physically strong	3	19
m)	Very fit and healthy	24	28
n)	Wealth	6	25
o)	Power and influence	1	8
	Don't know	2	5

IF MARRIED/LIVING WITH PARTNER. OTHERS GO TO Q16
Q15 I am going to read out a list of jobs which people have to do around the house. Please would you tell me who usually does each one, you or your husband/wife/partner or is it each of you equally? READ OUT. CODE BELOW

IF NOT LIVING WITH A HUSBAND/WIFE/PARTNER. OTHERS GO TO Q17
Q16 If you were married or living with someone as if you were married, which of you do you think would do each of these jobs, or do you think they would be split between you equally? READ OUT. CODE BELOW

		Husband/ Man %	Wife/ Woman %	Both equally %	Does not apply %
a)	Cleaning/housework	2	52	38	7
b)	Washing the dishes	13	30	47	10
c)	Gardening (if applic)	37	16	34	13
d)	Cooking	6	59	29	6
e)	Looking after the children (if applic)	1	25	31	43
f)	Decorating	44	10	33	13
g)	Household repairs/maintenance	71	2	13	13
h)	Paying Household Bills	33	25	35	7
i)	Who is/would be the main bread winner	67	6	18	9

TYPICALLY BRITISH?

- 8 -

ASK ALL

Q17 **What do you think are the main reasons people decide to get married these days?** DO NOT PROMPT. MULTICODE OK

	%
Because the woman is already pregnant	9
Companionship	22
Love	42
Religious reasons	1
Tax reasons/incentives/money	8
The opportunity for a special party/celebration	*
The wedding presents	*
To have children	21
To please their parents	2
Regular physical relationship/sex	3
Tradition/it's normal	11
Commitment to partner	10
Other (WRITE IN & AND CODE 1)	26
Don't know	12

Q18 **And what do you think are the main causes of divorce these days?** DO NOT PROMPT. MULTICODE OK.

	%
Boredom	5
Children	4
Drink	4
Growing apart	17
In–laws	*
Lack of money/financial problems	43
Lack of respect for each other	7
Poor sex life	2
Unfaithfulness	27
Violence	4
Other (WRITE IN & CODE 'X')	42
Don't know	6

Q19 SHOWCARD V (R) **How important do you think sexual love is in marriage?**

	%
Very important	37
Fairly important	47
Not very important	6
Not at all important	1
Don't know	8

Q20 SHOWCARD W (R) **How often do you have sexual intercourse these days?**

	%	
Four times a week or more	5	
Two or three times a week	19	
Once a week	13	ASK Q21
Once a fortnight	4	
Once a month	6	
Never	26	GO TO
Refused	15	Q 22
Don't know	11	

178

- 9 -

Q21 SHOWCARD X (R) **And how satisfying would you say sexual intercourse usually is for you?**

	%
Very satisfying	52
Fairly satisfying	44
Not very satisfying	2
Not at all satisfying	1
Refused	1
Don't know	1

ASK ALL

Q22 SHOWCARD F (R) **Now I'm going to read out some statements, and I'd like you to tell me to what extent you agree or disagree with each?** READ OUT. ALTERNATE ORDER.

TICK START (√)	Strongly agree %	Tend to agree %	Neither agree nor disagree %	Tend to disagree %	Strongly disagree %	No opinion %
a) A woman's place is in the home	7	14	15	29	35	1
b) The law should be changed to make it more difficult for people to get divorced	15	27	14	27	15	3
c) As long as no-one gets hurt, there's nothing wrong with extra-marital affairs	3	10	8	26	51	2
d) Most men do not do enough to share the housework	18	48	12	15	3	3
e) It's a bad idea for women to have children unless they are married	21	29	16	22	10	2
f) It's OK for unmarried people to have sex "just for the fun of it".	8	27	17	24	21	3
g) It is better to get married in a church than a registry office	17	24	32	15	10	2

179

Q23   SHOWCARD G (R) **Here is a list of things some people have said they have aspired to in life. I would like you to think back to the time when you were fifteen years old and tell me which, if any, of these things you wanted to do at some time in your life? Just read out the letters.** CODE BELOW

Q24   SHOWCARD G (R) AGAIN **And which have you actually done so far? Just read out the letters.** CODE BELOW

Q25   SHOWCARD G (R) AGAIN **And which do you expect you will do sometime during the rest of your life? Just read out the letters.** CODE BELOW

		Q23 %	Q24 %	Q25 %
a)	Get married	42	64	14
b)	Live with a partner without being married	2	14	4
c)	Have a son	8	25	3
d)	Have a daughter	7	24	2
e)	Have a son or a daughter	12	11	10
f)	Have two or more children of either sex	18	31	7
g)	Travel abroad	45	60	27
h)	Live abroad	10	10	9
i)	Speak a foreign language fluently	14	7	7
j)	Travel around the world	30	9	12
k)	Write a book	9	2	6
l)	Be in a cinema film	5	1	*
m)	Run your own business	21	13	11
n)	Meet a member of the Royal Family	4	8	1
o)	Become divorced	*	7	1
p)	Go to university/college	21	22	4
q)	Be on TV	5	5	1
r)	Fall in love	31	47	5
s)	Own your own home	37	49	14
t)	Learn to drive	48	57	8
u)	Own a sports car	19	10	7
v)	Represent your country in a sport	14	1	1
w)	Go into politics	3	1	1
x)	Become a millionaire	24	*	5
y)	Marry someone you knew when you were 15	8	6	1
z)	Learn to fly	8	1	3
aa)	Win the pools	28	3	11
	None of these	3	4	28
	No opinion	1	1	3

– 11 –

Q26   SHOWCARD H (R) Here is a list of different occupations that some people have said they wanted to do. Again thinking back to the time when you were fifteen years old please tell me which if any of these occupations you wanted to do. Just read out the letters.

Q27   SHOWCARD H (R) AGAIN And which have you actually done? Just read out the letters.

Q28   SHOWCARD H (R) AGAIN And which do you think you will do sometime during the rest of your life? Just read out the letters.

		Q26 %	Q27 %	Q28 %
a)	Accountant	4	2	1
b)	Artist	8	2	2
c)	Air Hostess/steward	11	*	*
d)	Airline Pilot	6	*	1
e)	Business Manager	3	4	3
f)	Doctor	4	*	*
g)	Factory Worker	2	17	2
h)	Fashion Model	5	1	1
i)	Fireman	4	1	1
j)	General Office Worker	3	11	2
k)	Insurance Salesman	1	1	1
l)	Lawyer	5	*	*
m)	Member of the Armed Forces	14	8	1
n)	Nun/Priest	2	*	*
o)	Nurse	16	6	3
p)	Policeman/policewoman	9	1	1
q)	Politician	1	*	*
r)	Pop Star	6	*	*
s)	Run your own business	17	12	14
t)	School Teacher	10	4	3
u)	Secretary	7	7	2
v)	Stockbroker	1	–	*
w)	Train Driver	4	*	*
x)	Other (WRITE IN AND CODE Y)	27	27	9
	None of these	12	26	56
	No opinion	2	1	3

Q29   SHOWCARD I (R) Now looking at this list of people and organisations, which, if any, would you say you are satisfied with in how they are performing their role in society? Just read out the letters.

Q30   SHOWCARD I (R) AGAIN And which, if any, are you dissatisfied with in how they are performing their role in society? Just read out the letters./

		Q29 Satisfied %	Q30 Dissatisfied %
a)	The Church	23	21
b)	Doctors	56	13
c)	Trade Unions	7	29
d)	The Police	36	26
e)	Parliament	7	39
f)	Civil Service	9	17
g)	The Royal Family	35	17
h)	Major Companies	10	14
i)	The Armed Forces	50	6
j)	Teachers	21	25
k)	The Legal System	11	31
l)	National Newspapers	11	30
m)	Government ministers	5	41
n)	Universities	19	8
o)	The BBC	23	18
p)	Independent Television	18	15
q)	Architects	8	15
r)	National Health Service (NHS)	25	45
	None of these	8	6
	No opinion	2	2

Q31 **Which of these – Europe, The Commonwealth, or America – is the most important to Britain?**

	%
Europe	54
Commonwealth	15
America	23
Don't know	8

Q32 **A number of ideas are being considered which, it is said, will bring the member states of the European Community closer together. Do you support or oppose the idea that . . . READ OUT. ALTERNATE ORDER.**

TICK (√) START

		Support %	Oppose %	No opinion %
☐	a) There should be a European passport instead of individual country passports	52	38	11
	b) There should be a fully integrated armed services to defend Europe	58	32	10
	c) More power should be transferred to the European Parliament from individual national Parliaments	30	54	16
	d) A Supreme Court of Europe should be introduced	45	38	18
☐	e) A Single European Currency should be introduced	44	46	10

Q32a SHOWCARD J (R) **Which of these places have you ever visited?**

	%
Australia	6
An African Country	14
Canada	10
An Eastern European Country	17
A Western European Country	66
India/Pakistan	7
The Republic of Ireland	16
Middle East	13
Far East	9
South America	3
United States of America	19
USSR/Soviet Union	2
Any other foreign country	16
None of these	16
No opinion	1

Q33 **Do you think Britain's membership of the Common Market over the past few years has or has not . . . READ OUT. ALTERNATE ORDER.**

TICK (√) START

		Has %	Has not %	No difference %	No Opinion
☐	a) Led to prices rising faster than they would have done	60	20	6	14
	b) Reduced Britain's control over her own destiny	62	24	5	10
	c) Given British industry greater opportunities	47	38	5	10
☐	d) Increased the political stability of Europe	51	26	6	17

CARD 3
SKIP COL

Q34 I am going to read out some things that people have said about America and Americans. Please tell me whether, on balance, you agree or disagree with each one? READ OUT. ALTERNATE ORDER.

TICK (√)START

		Agree %	Disagree %	Don't know %
☐	a) I like Americans as people	69	18	13
	b) I would like to go on holiday to America	69	29	2
	c) I think we can learn a great deal in this country from America	39	54	7
	d) I would like to live in America if I could not live in Britain	24	72	4
☐	e) We would be better off if we were more like the Americans in many respects	16	78	6

Q35 SHOWCARD K (R) Which, if any, of these have you been to in the past twelve months? Just read out the letters.

	%
a) Art Exhibition	23
b) Pop concert	17
c) Library	53
d) Theatre	36
e) Opera	6
f) Classical ballet	3
g) Museum	38
h) Modern dance	13
i) Orchestral concert	14
j) Cinema	44
k) Pantomime	15
l) Football match	19
m) National Trust house or garden	39
None	14
Don't know	*

Q36 SHOWCARD L (R) Which, if any, of the following things would you say you have done in the last year or two? Just read out the letters.

%

a) Been a member of an environmental group or
charity (even if you joined more than two years ago)............................ 12

b) Campaigned about an environmental issue.. 4

c) Given money to or raised money for wildlife, conservation
or Third World charities... 46

d) Read or watched TV about wildlife, conservation
natural resources or the Third World 77

e) Requested information from an organisation dealing
with wildlife, conservation, natural resources or the
Third World.. 13

f) Selected one product over another because of its
environmental–friendly packaging, formulation or
advertising... 46

g) Used unleaded petrol in your car 36

h) Subscribed to a magazine concerned with wildlife,
conservation, natural resources or the Third World.............................. 11

i) Visited or written a letter to an MP or Councillor about
wildlife, conservation, natural resources or the
Third World.. 10

j) Walked in the countryside or along the coast 79

k) Written a letter for publication to a newspaper about
wildlife, conservation, natural resources or the
Third World.. 3

l) Owned a pet 49

None of these 4
Don't know... *

Q37 SHOWCARD M (R) Which of these, if any, have you eaten in the last month?

%

Porridge 31
Bacon and eggs...72
Chinese meal 45
Indian meal 30
Hamburger...38
Pizza 52
Pasta..49
Sunday roast 84
Sausages 72
Fish and chips...74

None of these.. *
No opinion.. *

– 15 –

Q38 Are you a vegetarian or a vegan at present, or have you ever been a vegetarian or a vegan?

	%
Yes, vegetarian now	4
Yes, vegan now	1
Yes, vegetarian in the past	3
Yes, vegan in the past	*
No	92
Don't know	*

Q39 SHOWCARD N (R) And which, if any, of the things on this list have you done in the past two days? Just read out the appropriate letters.

	%
a) Eaten fresh fruit	78
b) Eaten wholemeal bread	60
c) Eaten fresh green vegetables	77
d) Eaten high fibre or wholemeal cereal	48
e) Had sugar in tea or coffee	46
f) Drunk a glass of whole milk	30
g) Had an alcoholic drink/beer/wine	47
h) Had fish and chips or a fry-up	33
i) Smoked a cigarette, pipe or cigar	31
j) Taken part in a team sport (eg football, cricket)	8
k) Taken part in an individual sport or exercise	22
l) Taken marijuana or other drugs	1
m) Taken any medicine	30
n) Been on a diet to lose weight	14
o) Taken vitamin pills	16
p) Taken painkiller (eg aspirin/paracetamol)	32
None of these	*

Q40 SHOWCARD O (R) Which of the things on this card have you done in the past month? Just read out the appropriate letters.

	%
a) Competitive sport	14
b) General exercise/keep fit	37
c) Been to a wine bar(s)	10
d) DIY	38
e) Gardening	56
f) Been out for a Sunday afternoon drive	37
g) Been to pub(s)	46
h) Been to the cinema	20
i) Been to the theatre	12
j) Watched TV/Video	90
k) Had friends round to your home for a meal or drink	48
l) Been to a nightclub/disco	13
m) Placed a bet on a dog or horse	18
n) Gone for a run/jog	8
o) Played billiards/snooker/pool	16
p) Been away for the weekend	22
q) Been to a sports club	13
r) Been to a social/working men's club	14
s) Been away on holiday	12
t) Been to a restaurant	44
u) Had a meal from a takeaway/fast food outlet	43
v) Been to a zoo	4
w) Been to an amusement/video game arcade	7
x) Gone shopping for food	84
y) Read nutritional information on food labels	30
z) Read a book	63
aa) Made your own beer or wine	2
None of these	*
Don't know	*

Q41 SHOWCARD P (R) I am going to read out a list of statements some people have made. For each one would you please tell me how strongly you agree or disagree with each statement. READ OUT. ROTATE ORDER

TICK START (√)	Strongly agree %	Tend to agree %	Neither agree nor disagree %	Tend to disagree %	Strongly disagree %	No opinion %
a) Britain should keep its nuclear weapons even if other countries get rid of theirs	15	24	9	26	21	4
b) Having a healthy diet is important to me	45	42	7	3	1	2
c) Food additives should be banned	25	34	21	15	2	3
d) Britain has lost its role in the world	14	34	14	27	6	4
e) If I had the opportunity to emigrate I'd take it	9	15	12	29	23	2
f) Britain is now a classless society	3	10	9	38	37	3
g) I expect Britain to be engaged in another war within the next ten years	6	33	21	24	11	6
h) Smoking in public places should be banned	40	26	10	14	9	1
i) The British like their pets more than their relatives	10	36	13	18	6	16

Q42 Generally speaking, do you think of yourself as Conservative, Labour, Liberal Democrat, or what?

	%
Conservative	31
Labour	32
Liberal Democrat	14
Scot/Welsh Nat	1
Green Party	2
Other	1
None	10
Undecided	6
Refused	3

Q43 Have you always lived within about ten miles of here, or have you ever lived somewhere else?

	%
Always lived around here	48
Lived somewhere else	51

Q44   SHOWCARD Q (R) May I ask which of the things on this list you have done in the last two
or three years? Just read out the appropriate letters.

%
a) Presented my views to local councillor or MP 15
b) Written a letter to an editor 5
c) Urged someone outside my family to vote 17
d) Urged someone to get in touch with a local
councillor or MP 16
e) Made a speech before an organised group 15
f) Been elected an officer of an organisation or club.................................. 13
g) Stood for public office 1
h) Taken an active part in a political campaign.. 3
i) Helped on fund raising drives 32
j) Voted in last election.. 66
None of these 19

Q45   What was the natural colour of your hair when you were fifteen?

%
Black... 7
Dark Brown 28
Brown 21
Light Brown... 16
Fair.. 10
Blonde.. 11
Ginger/redhead 5
Other (WRITE IN AND CODE '8') 2

....
No opinion.. 1

THANK RESPONDENT.   GO TO DEMOGRAPHICS THEN ASK RESPONDENT FEEDBACK
QUESTIONS AT THE END OF THE QUESTIONNAIRE.

INDEX